FALLING THROUGH TRAPDOORS

A Television Adventure

Bob Harvey

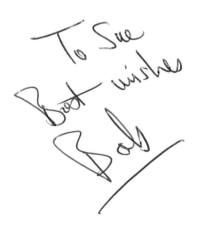

To Sue
Best wishes
Bob

Falling Through Trapdoors

© Bob Harvey 2019

Spellcaster Publishing

ISBN   9781795556859

Also by Bob Harvey:
How To Make Your Own Video Or Short Film
www.amazon.co.uk and all good book stores.

For Jane

ACKNOWLEDGEMENTS

I am indebted to numerous people for the contributions they made to my chequered career; the many technicians without whose generosity, patience and professionalism I would never have made it through the labyrinth of obstacles waiting to mug me; the roll-call of producers who were happy to assign me to projects, often on a wing and a prayer and without any apparent regard for their own reputations or sanity, most notably Dan Maddicott, Michael Rodd, Jill Roach, Nigel Pope, Clive Moffatt, Chas Lister and Helen Eisler; Dave Wood for letting me loose in the backstreets of Newcastle with four heavy metal bands, a sledgehammer and a van load of pyrotechnics; Alan Afriat for allowing me to document our involuntary collaboration in almost extinguishing Teddington Studios – an act of demolition only achieved in later years by Time's reckless abandonment of one of our most beloved broadcasting institutions; to all the actors, presenters and clients who had to endure my moments of creative whimsy, and to my wife who accompanied me on my journey without once suggesting I might like to try my hand at something that was less of a magnet for those with accident-prone tendencies.

ALONG THE HIGH WIRE

There can surely be no purpose in life more satisfying than to fulfil an ambition for which you have a passion. For me it was to work in television and forge a career as a director. Considering the broadcasting industry is over-subscribed, unpredictable, and a minefield of creative conflict, it is remarkable that I seriously embarked on it as a vocation. When I look back on a journey that took me halfway around the world, filming with a multitude of human egos, on perilous mountain roads, in shipyards, factories and various other hazardous environments, surrounded by expensive equipment, electricity cables, pyrotechnics and water, it seems incredible that I emerged unscathed to tell the tale. By immense good fortune I did survive and so present my rocky ride through the telly trade in all its buttock-clenching, nerve-jangling reminiscence, complete with behind-the-scenes revelations, exposés and encounters with, among others, Sir Laurence Olivier, The Beatles, Hughie Green, Jonathan Routh, Marty Feldman, Jim Davidson, Lenny Henry, Fred Housego, Sir George Martin, Chris Evans, Larry Grayson, Keith Harris, Josie Lawrence, James Fleet, Frank Bruno, Dennis the Menace, Superman and The Dulux Dog.

THE AUTHOR

Bob Harvey has worked on a diverse range of television programmes, from *Candid Camera* to *The World at War, Horizon* to *The Spice of Life*. As a writer/director his career has encompassed documentary, drama, children's, light entertainment and current affairs and includes *The Animal Magic Show, Olympic Hall of Fame, Stagestruck, Timebusters* and *The Six O'Clock Show*. His book *How to Make Your Own Video Or Short Film* was published in 2008 and in between broadcast assignments he tutored film-making courses at Ravensbourne Media College and the Met Film School at Ealing Studios. In 2004 he received a BAFTA for his directing work on BBC TV's *Raven* series.

RITE OF PASSAGE

In the spring of 1975, I found myself waiting with trepidation outside the apartment of the most celebrated *enfant terrible* of the broadcasting industry, the entertainer Hughie Green. I had heard about Hughie's reputation and his ability to humiliate and terrify all who crossed his path and suspected he could be incredibly difficult, if not impossible, to work with, so when asked if I would like to direct a car commercial featuring the infamous celebrity I was naturally guarded. I had to balance my apprehension, however, with my desire to put some much needed directing experience under my belt, so I agreed to meet up with him at his apartment in Baker Street. Before setting off, however, I invested some time reading up on Hughie's background so that I might at least appear suitably knowledgeable, and was surprised at what I discovered.

Hughie was a former child star who, at the age of fourteen, had appeared in numerous low budget British films and formed Hughie Green's Gang, a touring revue show that gave exposure to new young talent. He produced over seven hundred shows in one year alone, employed a hundred and fifty support staff, and earned £20,000 a year at a time when the average wage was just £1 a day. He was the biggest teen star Britain ever produced, and at the age of seventeen was signed up to make cinema films in Hollywood, with the offer of a further five-year contract. To his parents' dismay Hughie turned down the offer and chose instead to join up and support the war effort and as an accomplished pilot, flew missions from North America to Europe delivering aircraft. Since the crews had to fly across the Atlantic they were sitting ducks for the German air force and one in four of the planes never made it.

After the war, Hughie returned to the entertainment world, developing *Opportunity Knocks* as a radio show before moving over to the then recently formed ITV to present *Double Your Money*, which utilised his unique ability to interact with the general public and became one of the highest rating audience shows ever between 1955 and 1968. By the late sixties he was one of the biggest names in broadcasting, his newly revived *Opportunity Knocks* now a television format giving a springboard to many of the country's top comedians and singers, and attracting over sixteen million viewers a week.

But there was a darker side to Hughie, one that threatened to tarnish his reputation as Mr Popular as he began to acquire more and more media power. In his business dealings he could be ruthless and unforgiving; he was a known womaniser, and by all accounts could be as cruel as he could be compassionate.

And so it was that I found myself outside his Baker Street flat one afternoon, fearful of how our meeting might progress. What I hadn't realised was that Hughie had been lost at sea in his boat during a storm and no contact had been made for several days. I recalled that in 1961 his yacht *Rakes Retreat* had met with difficulties picking up a mooring buoy in Friar's Bay and had to be towed to safety, but this second incident seemed an altogether more serious occurrence. There had been articles about his disappearance in the national press but for some reason these had escaped my attention. His Scottish housekeeper gave no indication of the drama that had been unfolding as she showed me into the living room and I waited a good twenty minutes before he eventually shuffled in to meet me. I was taken aback.

He was slightly hunched, had several days' growth of white stubble on his chin and was dressed in just a grubby white vest and a pair of loose-fitting underpants. He had also been drinking heavily and was grasping a small whisky glass in his hand. It was immediately obvious that Hughie wasn't altogether himself, possibly still traumatised. The events of the past week and his near-death experience had clearly taken its toll and here I was, proving to be the master of bad timing. I immediately wanted to leave but Hughie waved a hand at an armchair and I duly sat down, wondering how we were going to have a meaningful conversation under the circumstances.

He replenished his glass and sat in front of me, his eyes glazed, his hands unsteady. I had only ever seen him as the smartly dressed, self-assured, twinkly-eyed man smiling and brimming with confidence on a television screen, so this was altogether something of a culture shock. He rambled on for some minutes about not having had time to get his papers together and although at first I thought he meant his script notes for the commercial, it transpired he thought I was from the insurance company, sent to deal with his claim for compensation for his wrecked boat. In that respect I considered myself rather fortunate, though I would have given anything to be a fly on the wall during *that* particular conversation.

Having put him straight on why I was there, he launched into a lengthy deliberation on the shortcomings of the vehicle he was meant to be promoting, then went off at an odd tangent to talk about his schooldays. Halfway through this rendition, and just as I thought things couldn't get any worse, he swung his right leg over the chair arm and his tackle slid away from inside his underpants and came to rest in a more prominent position in my direct line of sight. He was completely oblivious to the urgent rearrangement that was needed to his clothing and as the conversation wore on it became increasingly difficult for me to take him seriously. I tried to put things back on track by telling him how impressed I was with the anti-corrosion warranty the car manufacturers were giving but he dismissed this with a brusque 'that's a load of rubbish, old son, not worth the paper it's written on,' and drifted into a political debate, littered with profanities, which involved the McCarthy era in America. The meeting came to an abrupt end when he decided I wasn't being terribly sympathetic to his political affiliations and his housekeeper showed me to the door. A few days later I heard that the car commercial had been cancelled, the advertising agency probably having decided that showing their latest model being test driven by a man who couldn't even navigate a boat around the Isle of Wight was probably not one of their better ideas.

When he had fully recovered from the ordeal, Hughie went to great lengths to make amends, inviting me to supper and asking me to direct a documentary he was making on behalf of British Airways called *First Flight*, about a group of travellers flying abroad for the first time. I recalled that he had gone missing in a plane some years prior to the boating fiasco and that particular story had also occupied a fair amount of column inches. Undeterred I agreed to make the film and it passed without incident, proving that perhaps there is a God of Good Intent after all. In fact, I quite warmed to Hughie for all his faults and found the few get-togethers we shared quite illuminating as he opened up and shared private thoughts that in many respects I felt he probably should have kept to himself. On one occasion he even confessed that although he liked the occasional drink, his real weakness was with the fair sex, the details of which discretion prohibits further discussion, but it became an obsession that was to cause a great deal of friction and unhappiness in his life, and for the many who became involved in his carnal pursuits.

Hughie may have been a selfish monster to many who knew him, but one event that summed up his mass appeal occurred one morning when we were parked in his Bentley on a double yellow line, in Central London, occupying the space of two normal cars. An officious looking traffic warden in his midfifties tapped on the side window and peered in with a look of disdain. Hughie wound down the window, beamed a smile and said: 'It's okay, old son, it's only me,' to which the warden replied, 'Oh, I'm terribly sorry, Mr Green, I didn't realise it was you in there. Sorry to have bothered you.' The warden saluted and continued on his way without the slightest suggestion that we might consider moving on, and I realised I had witnessed something rather extraordinary; on a par perhaps with Obi Wan Kanobi's telepathic abilities to persuade a Stormtrooper to accede to his wishes without putting up the slightest resistance. In an age of celebrity obsession that was going to take some beating.

His position of prominence in the public eye was not destined to last, however. As Hughie took increasing advantage of his fame he began to upset his department heads with his refusal to adapt to the demands of an evolving broadcast environment, and his career slid into gradual decline. Right up until its final show, *Opportunity Knocks* attracted up to eighteen million viewers weekly but Hughie, known for his right-wing politics, had decided he was bigger than the show's format and began politicising the accepted family-friendly format. He even used *Opportunity Knocks* as an end-of-year soapbox, telling the country at the end of 1974 to 'Stand Up and Be Counted'. He was disciplined by Thames Television, but continued to make political comments and after numerous viewer complaints, Thames axed the show in March 1978. After that, things went from bad to worse. He lost a court case against the New Zealand Broadcasting Corporation over a copyright issue which cost him £250,000 and was forced to live out his life away from the media spotlight in relative solitude, without many of the financial riches of his former fame, and died of cancer in the Royal Marsden Hospital in 1997.

To dismiss Hughie Green as a selfish egomaniac would be to seriously under-value his role in the development of British television. He certainly courted controversy and outrage, particularly in his later years, but there is no question that he gave opportunities to hundreds of singers, dancers and comedians as well as pioneering the game show format as we know it today. Beneath the brash exterior he harboured a love of show business and respect for the country that had elevated him to celebrity status, even though it had paradoxically bestowed on him a unique power that was to eventually destroy him. Hughie's story is, in many ways, a story of our times, yet it gave me the opportunity, as a young fledgling director, to see at first hand the conflicting and contrasting elements of an industry that anyone who has the desire to become a part of might be advised to approach with a mixture of passion and immense caution.

It was one of many episodes I would take heed of on my journey through the creative minefield of the British television industry; a culmination of events, as rich and varied as they were unexpected and enlightening; a treasure trove of discovery that I would come to cherish and look back on with great satisfaction and affection.

MAGIC CARPET

A career in television seemed a world away when I was at school. State establishments in the sixties were neither equipped nor favourably disposed to cater for the kind of airy-fairy ambitions that involved the creative arts, unless by courtesy of the school choir, the brass band, or a yearly costume drama awash with historical illumination.

As a tall gangly lad of thirteen, impaired vision played a significant role in my inability to tread the boards in school productions, and my numerous auditions wearing NHS glasses for period dramas such as *Julius Caesar* or *Don Quixote* at Chase Cross Secondary Modern in Romford invariably came to grief as I bumbled about the stage, colliding with props and fellow actors before falling into the makeshift orchestra pit. Although relegated to less dangerous backstage tasks such as opening and closing the curtains, playing in the sound effects and running the school radio station, I soon discovered these activities to be the most motivational part of school life and became fixated with the idea of embracing the technical side of creative media as a possible calling.

I would never have dreamt that in the following years, on contract with the major UK broadcasters, I would come close to being blown sky high by a heavy metal band's pyrotechnics in Newcastle, escape by inches being mown down by a rally car in Corsica, be detained and blacklisted by customs at Heathrow Airport, fall down the hold of a container vessel in Gothenburg port, spend a fortnight in Weston-Super-Mare with an army of dwarves running rampage through the town dressed as space aliens, and be accused of setting fire to the Thames TV studios in Teddington.

These are but a handful of incidents I can bring myself to think about without the need to reach for a cold compress, and I often feel a sense of trepidation when I meet up with old film crew mates from the past who rekindle scary memories, long forgotten, when they start by saying 'Do you remember that time…'

I wouldn't, of course, change a single moment. At the age of seventeen I had stepped onto a magic carpet that offered a myriad of experiences; a carpet that must have been fire-proof, water-proof and idiot-proof, since I invariably tripped over it, fell off it, or found myself holding on for dear life as it hurtled around without any apparent sense of direction. Yet it took me to some wondrous places and introduced me to some amazing people; some famous, some with immense courage, others who have left exceptional legacies, yet all of whom shaped and invigorated an extraordinary and unforgettable journey. And despite the many obstacles that littered my path during forty years of working in the telly trade I somehow, against all the odds, managed to prove that if you have the passion and commitment, you can achieve almost anything.

None of this can, of course, be achieved alone and it would be foolish to believe otherwise. Being passionate about your work is one thing, but rallying the support of colleagues who believe in your talents ultimately becomes crucial to your eventual success and in that respect the TV industry is no different from any other, even though many might see it as a privileged workplace residing on the edge of fantasy land. It is only natural that people should generally underestimate the pressure and stress experienced by those working within the film and television environment, even if during the course of a normal working day nobody is expected to administer a colonoscopy, perform a heart transplant, make decisions that can seal the fate of an entire continent, or take responsibility for halting the collapse of our global financial infrastructure. Despite the fact that most media practitioners are well paid for their varied roles as opinion formers, educators and creators of roller-coaster entertainment, the images of glamour, fun and excitement presented to the general public invariably mask the fact that it can be a volatile, erratic and insecure industry. It's a business that takes few prisoners as it throws people of all ages, genders and skills into a melting pot of creative differences and personality clashes, pushed to the limit through outrageously long hours, with the participants often surviving on a cocktail of adrenaline and ego. In such situations it is hardly surprising that questionable social distractions and practices often seep into the lives of those trapped in a relentless cycle of expectation, many having been forced to jockey for position in a highly competitive freelance market in order to survive occupational meltdown.

Television has endured more than eighty-five years of cultural change and constant technological and budgetry readjustment yet it has always retained its ability to attract some of the most hard-working, colourful and eccentric characters anyone could have the good fortune to work with. During the years I spent learning my craft at a variety of studios and locations spread all over the world, it is the time I spent with this collection of disparate individuals that brings the widest of smiles to my face. Because no matter where we have found ourselves and whatever productions we have been engaged on, the crew are ultimately the ones who provide the inspiration, enlightenment and laughter to keep everyone sane when the walls start caving in.

When you think about it, how could it be any different? Being stuck on a Polar ice cap with only penguins and turtles for company for six months would be enough to turn anyone loopy, and finding yourself marooned on a desert island trying to complete a drama with limited time and on a miniscule budget would be intolerable without the support of a loyal bunch of pros; even more essential if the actors are constantly bickering and the days alternate between unforgiving sun and raging monsoon. Or being on the road for a month with four Heavy Metal bands whose primary objective seems to be to destroy your ear-drums or maim you for life with van-loads of volatile pyrotechnics (more of which later).

11

When you live your days in a parallel universe that often doesn't have even half a foot in reality, you are thankful for the support - both technical and moral - of comrades in arms who can remain calm under the most trying of conditions and retain their sense of humour, whatever is thrown at them. So when the equipment goes down, you know they will fix it with the minimum of fuss and bother. When you take a wrong turning and find yourselves lost in the middle of nowhere you can put your faith and trust in an extraordinary intuition that will get everyone back on track, without the need to study a map or plug in a SatNav. And their knowledge of the world around them never ceases to astound and amaze. Sitting around a table taking supper with a film crew can open up your eyes to a world of jaw-dropping, non-stop, information that is beyond your personal biscuit-tin of knowledge.

'Did you know that manufacturers print invisible yellow dots on consumer's photocopies that check to see if a person is printing counterfeit money?'

'No, I *didn't* know that'.

'Or that one of the oldest micronations, the republic of Molossia in Nevada is inhabited by only four citizens? Founded in May 1977 and formerly known as the republic of Vuldnstein, it has its own railway and issues currency.'

'Get *out* of here!'

'It's a fact. And if anyone from Molossia farts consistently for four years and nine months, enough gas is produced to create the energy of an atom bomb.'

And so it goes on, unrelentingly, into the night until your brain can't take any more and you seek the refuge of a sound-proofed room and a comfortable bed.

'If your DNA was stretched out it would reach the moon six thousand times... If the population of China walked past you in single file, the line would never end because of the rate of reproduction... Did you know that more than twelve people are killed each year by vending machines?'...

I'm not saying all of this is information is *useful* information but it certainly stimulates discussion and adds to an evening's entertainment value. And no matter how exhausted everyone is when bed-time beckons, that same crew will be up at the crack of dawn next morning, first at the location ready for a day's work. A remarkable bunch I feel privileged to have been in the company of for so many years.

Not everyone in telly land is quite so supportive and obliging of course. Where there are differences of opinion and unbridled personal ambition there will always be discord and conflict. Whilst I would love to paint a rosy picture of eternal friendship and harmonious mutual admiration, the truth is that the television industry can often be more cut-throat and unforgiving than most and it would certainly be foolhardy, not to say naïve, for anyone involved in it to step along their elected career path without checking the ground for trap-doors every so often.

And if there were trap-doors within a mile of me you could bet your life I would find them.

INTO THE UNKNOWN

When I took my first tentative steps into the madcap world of film and television in the mid-1960s, London found itself at the centre of the universe. Carnaby Street boasted a surfeit of 'hip' clothes shops that attracted the beautiful and the famous, ladies of the night hung out of windows from various apartments in Soho, and the theatres were gearing up to stage risqué productions such as *Oh Calcutta!* and *Hair,* which would reflect, with neither modesty nor subtlety, the hippie culture and sexual revolution of the times. Back in those heady but relatively innocent days, Peter Cook and Dudley Moore were rocking the establishment, *Private Eye* had begun firing broadsides at the government of the day, and Beatlemania was in full swing, bringing with it changing attitudes that would affect the social fabric of western society and become a cultural phenomenon.

To a greenhorn full of hope and ambition, this was an exciting time to set out on a voyage through the creative arts. In my first job as a runner with James Garrett and Partners, a commercials production company based in New Bond Street, I rubbed shoulders with some of the most innovative and influential directors of the day. Richard Lester, Joe McGrath, David Bailey, Ken Russell and a roll-call of cinema directors had been engaged to apply their extensive talents to the selling of a vast range of consumables. These ranged from soap powder to chocolate bars, toilet rolls to hair sprays, the advertising agencies forever experimenting with new ideas to tempt the public into parting with their cash for products they didn't know they wanted or needed.

The first television commercial, for Gibbs SR toothpaste, was transmitted on September 22nd 1955, and by the early sixties the manipulative conventions of on-screen advertising had been firmly established. The Dulux Dog (who many years later was to play a part in one of my most bizarre shoots), made his first foray into the wacky world of advertising the same year I joined Garretts, becoming a part of the branding process that had immediate and immense purchasing power. Catchy slogans and musical jingles also played their part. The Smarties adverts ended with a small child tunefully asking us to 'Buy some for Lulu,' a completely meaningless lyric that we nevertheless all walked around singing, along with 'Don't forget the Fruit Gums, Mum,' and 'You'll wonder where the yellow went when you brush your teeth with Pepsodent.' The trick was to create image systems and sounds that stayed with you and penetrated your subconscious. Branding was everything. We were encouraged by Esso to put a tiger in our tanks and by the Egg Marketing Board to go to work on an egg, whilst a bunch of Martians promoted instant Smash, persuading us that we no longer had to endure the laborious task of peeling potatoes. Advertising worked, and worked incredibly well, and by the time I took up gainful employment with Garretts, advertising had reached extraordinary levels of refinement, with thirty-second commercials having been transformed into a compelling and seductive art form.

A gateway of possibility stretched before me as my magic carpet swept along the pavements and side streets of London, at a time when anything was possible and money seemed never in short supply. Commercials were made on astonishingly generous budgets and the James Garrett offices often resembled a mini warehouse as crates of whisky and cigarettes from grateful account managers were delivered on a regular basis. During the Christmas period, when 'entertaining the client' was placed high on the festive agenda, creative directors and production personnel disappeared for hours on end to attend non-stop parties and drinks sessions. Not that any of them were neglecting their creative responsibilities of course; they just put them on hold during the festive season whilst rosy-cheek syndrome - all in the worthy cause of keeping the clients happy - pervaded the corridors and meeting rooms.

As a new recruit I stood very much on the periphery of all this, dreaming of the day when recognition would come and I too could indulge in the fruits of my artistic labours. In the meantime, whilst the cream of British film-making basked in the festive limelight, I carried on with the rather more mundane duties of cataloguing film trims in the vaults, fetching teas and coffees, and delivering daily rushes and completed films to agencies and laboratories within a five-mile radius of New Bond Street. Carrying wobbly piles of 35mm film cans around London with my knees buckling under the weight was a tricky business. Today a runner or a courier can deliver an entire two-hour movie on a DVD weighing the equivalent of a bag of feathers. In 1965 a movie was housed inside a dozen film cans you could hardly pick up without the aid of a fork-lift truck and afforded every possibility for calamitous incident as I staggered through the streets of the capital trying to deliver them within a set time scale. I see no purpose in recalling the near-misses I had with buses, taxis and pedestrians as I strained to see above the towering stacks. Thankfully nobody was seriously injured and the handful of cans that did meet a premature and mangled end did not, by some miracle, contain any film that was irreplaceable.

A year after joining Garretts I realised that running around the West End ducking and diving catastrophe was not a fast-track route to success – especially without a union card, the golden ticket that was essential if you were to be given meaningful employment in the film industry. In the mid-sixties the ACTT was a powerful organisation. Its General Secretary, Alan Sapper, was a militant who gave little ground in negotiations, and shop stewards could bring studios to a sudden and grinding halt at the click of a finger. Without a union card your career had no chance of even getting to first base. No union card no job, no job no union card, a circle of inconvenience that was hard to crack. For me the answer was to join Filmatic film laboratory in West London as a trainee technician, a role that guaranteed instant acceptance into the union, even though it meant another year of clawing my way patiently towards creative fulfilment, working long hours in dark rooms where only infra-red light offered any visual clues to stop me bumping into work benches or falling into developing tanks that smelled of strong vinegar and hit the back of my throat with startling ferocity whenever I walked past them. And made your eyes water.

It didn't take long for the management to realise that as a lad of immense naivety and inexperience I might be a potential danger to myself and others if allowed too much exposure to toxic chemicals and hazardous materials so I was drafted to a safer area of the laboratory devoted to the viewing and checking of processed films.

Examining films as they rolled off the production line proved to be a real treat. There was so much variety, from old Charlie Chaplin movies for the 8mm home market, to Harrison Marks specials for connoisseurs of the naked flesh. Marks' films of nubile young women in the nude playing tennis or taking character roles in films such as *One Track Mind, Dream Goddess* and *Come Play With Me* were celebrated in clubs, dormitories, bedrooms and more dubious establishments throughout the land, one of the few sources of moving imagery displaying tits and bums with the occasional glimpse of pubic hair that you could legally acquire. All very innocent and laughable to today's internet-savvy voyeurs, but popular enough in their day for hundreds of 'damaged' copies to be spirited out of the laboratory dump-bin for distribution to glamour-hungry collectors, not all of whom wore dirty macs and shuffled about in darkened alleyways. There was a growing body of opinion, in fact, that rallied to the cause of lifting accepted moral taboos, not just those related to sexual awakening but in the entire field of self-expression.

In the summer of 1966, a young unknown Japanese artist and experimental filmmaker, Yoko Ono, arrived on the laboratory's doorstep with a large pile of unprocessed 16mm film showing close-ups of naked bottoms as they walked along a treadmill. Her film, *No.4*, would become a talking point among the artists and auters on the London and New York scene, helping to elevate her to artistic prominence. For a bunch of laboratory technicians who were not privy to this inner circle of creative acclamation, the daily ritual of sitting in a darkened room watching an endless parade of human buttocks in perpetual motion seemed to be a pointless, if not altogether weird experience. Thankfully when England won the World Cup in the same year our attention was diverted from the eternal cavalcade of nipples and spotty bums to the patriotic fervour that had gripped the nation. The match proved to be a real gold mine for the laboratory, since the original TV transmission had only been broadcast in black and white. Colour copies of the game poured off the production line in a veritable cascade, keeping us in gainful employment for months, the defective copies becoming a valuable commodity, with no shortage of takers.

After a further twelve months of getting nowhere slowly in dark, pungent, windowless rooms, I was offered a job as a trainee assistant film editor at Athos Films in Soho, the only credential required for acceptance being my much coveted union card, which I had duly upgraded from 'Laboratory Assistant' to 'Production'. The company assigned me to a series of excruciatingly dull academic programmes designated for BBC afternoon broadcast spots that viewers came across more by accident than design. *Engineering Today, Level 2 Algebra* and *Molecular Genetics* provided neither a measurable amount of stimulation nor motivation, but at least I had a foot in the door. Back in the sixties there were hundreds of film cutting rooms spread throughout London, manned by jobbing editors who spent much of their time discussing, criticising and dissecting the work of eminent filmmakers such as Hitchcock, Fellini and Truffaut, whilst committing their own skills to the thankless and sometimes desperate task of making educational films for the government seem inspiring and thought-provoking. Whilst today's comedians parody such early training films as *How to Spot a Communist Infiltrator, Fifty-Six Ways to Position a Ladder* and *Avoiding Electrocution in the Workplace*, it's a sobering thought that these presentations were taken deadly seriously in the fifties and sixties, even if today they appear quaint in their execution.

Whatever their level of competence and professionalism, film editors upheld a strict code of conduct, with cutting room etiquette requiring an assistant editor or trainee to observe creative activity from a distance, sat on a chair filing film trims, but never offering comment, or stepping into the work area occupied by the editor unless requested to do so.

My first few weeks were particularly uninspiring as I tried to learn the ropes but without any real incentive, tolerating days of non-existent social intercourse with my editor, who grunted with annoyance if the edit wasn't going well, or chuckled if something that we were not destined to share, tickled his fancy.

On one occasion a film trim of two frames, less than the size of a postage stamp, went missing and despite an extensive hunt I failed to locate it anywhere. 'You stay here until you find it,' were my instructions as he slipped on his jacket at six o'clock and set off for home. I scoured every inch of his work bench, and the floor beneath, hoping it was him who was culpable, but to no avail. In desperation I hunted through my sandwich box, my trouser turn-ups, and for a third time rummaged through the trim bin where all the film off-cuts were hung, since some of the little buggers occasionally fell from their tiny pegs and hid at the bottom. No luck there either. Tired and dispirited I called it a day and headed home, resolved to declaring my incompetence in the morning and being prepared for the worst. As I sat down in my living room and slipped off one of my shoes, a small piece of celluloid fell onto the carpet - the missing two frames, staring up at me as a warning that the search for a stray film trim can never be extensive enough.

The next day, I arrived in the cutting room bright and early, placed the film trim on the editor's workbench and waited for his grateful reaction. When he eventually bowled in he simply picked it up and inserted it into his edit without so much as a word of thanks or a grunt of appreciation. I know where *I'd* like to have inserted it.

During the following weeks I became desperate to escape my dispiriting daily grind with such a pompous arse, until one morning my immediate destiny was taken unexpectedly out of my hands. After a viewing of our current work-in-progress the producer turned to me and asked what I thought of the film, rendering me momentarily speechless. The producer asking *my* opinion! I can't remember my exact response, something along the lines of it being very interesting, though I found a couple of the scenes a little confusing. I knew immediately from the look that passed between them that this was not what either of them wanted to hear. The cheek of it; a trainee suggesting there was a lack of clarity within their programme that had the potential to confuse the viewer. I made a mental note that in future if any editor asked me for my opinion the least I could do would be to perform a couple of double somersaults and offer nothing less than gushing outpourings of praise.

The next morning, I found myself mysteriously drafted down to Tunnel Films in Old Compton Street, Soho, to work with another editor on a programme with the slash-your-wrists title of *Electromagnetic Coursework*. Many of the London based film production companies rented rooms that were converted into overflow cutting rooms; such was the demand by cinema and TV audiences at that time. The difference with my new posting was that I had to fight my way in and out of work each day past a crowd of excited girls who were parked on the stairwell, a direct result of my cutting room being next door to my new neighbours, The Beatles, who were editing their fantasy musical *Magical Mystery Tour*.

When my new editor took off on two weeks' leave and left me to log his rushes, I found it impossible to give the work my full concentration when the Beatles and their entourage were having so much fun next door. As a result, my daily routine began to suffer, compounded by the constant noise of chattering girls emanating from the stairwell and the problem of having to wheel a trolley laden with large and heavy film cans around a growing number of bodies that had gathered on the landing. This included, on several occasions, John and Ringo, who took to playing Cowboys and Indians whenever they tired of being movie moguls, which seemed to be most of the time. I did at least manage to avoid burying them under piles of weighty, wobbling film cans on several occasions, though John always eyed me with a mixture of sympathy and caution whenever I weaved around a corner trundling my creaking trolley. When he asked me what film I was working on I told him it was a pop promo for the Dave Clark Five, though he might have wondered why there was a distinct lack of music emanating from my cutting room, just the occasional crackle and sparkle of electrically charged particles that formed the basis of visual demonstrations for *Electromagnetic Coursework*. I would love to have met George during my time at Tunnel Films but he seldom made an appearance, though Paul did pop in periodically to use my phone (he didn't have his own for some reason), but never stopped long enough to join me for a cup of tea and a digestive.

It was exciting to have occupied the Beatles' personal cosmic space for a short time, even though the end result of their labours was somewhat disappointing. Although The Beatles had worked with director Richard Lester on their two previous films, *A Hard Day's Night* and *Help!* and must have been heavily influenced by his abstract use of imagery, without his guiding hand it was not destined for the same critical acclaim. Although the film, broadcast on the BBC over the 1967 Christmas holidays, was received with varying levels of debate and conjecture, my experiences during the post-production phase are ones that I will always treasure, the music guaranteed to live on when the film itself may have faded in the memory.

By January 1968, Athos Films decided that I had not been giving my full attention to *Electromagnetic Coursework* when several rolls of rushes went missing, located a few days later at Kings Cross Lost Property Office as a result of me leaving them on the Tube. When the company bid me a not-so-fond farewell I had learnt my first hard lesson: that adopting a professional attitude was not just essential, it was everything if I was to have any chance of achieving success. I realised it was time to place my creative heroes on the backburner for a while and face up to the realities of furthering my career through pure hard graft and focus, no matter what disrespect or indifference was accorded me by those I was assigned to work with.

My next port of call was a fortuitous apprenticeship with two well established and highly regarded film editors, Stan Hawkes and Arthur Solomon, whose company Radius Films was based in Endell Street near Covent Garden. Stan and Arthur worked with some of the top directors of their day, editing a rich and varied series of broadcast documentaries, from *Anything Can Happen*, a film following raw police recruits as they took to the streets for the first time, to *One Pair of Eyes*, a quirky observation on British life as seen through the surreal mind of comedian Marty Feldman.

The learning curve was tremendous; a memorable association that gave me my first real grounding in the techniques of film editing. Stan and Arthur had no pretensions about their roles in the scheme of things and nurtured no desire to become heavyweight producers or entrepreneurs, being generous to a fault with their encouragement and advice. Within a year I had stepped up from trainee to assistant editor, helped by these two experienced editors who paved the way for my entry into the hallowed corridors of the BBC and ITV.

It was a journey that would be sprinkled with moments of despair and elation, joy and tragedy, yet I always remained vigilant in my efforts not to be side-tracked by company politics and creative differences, resolving instead to stay focused as I edged my way along the precarious high wire.

TOUCHDOWN

When I arrived at Ealing Studios for the first time in the autumn of 1968, the BBC had invested heavily in updating the sound stages and cutting rooms where the acclaimed Ealing comedies had once been made, and were in full production on dramas and documentaries. At its peak, 56 film crews used the studios as a base for location filming of dramas such as *Cathy Come Home* and *Z-Cars* and there were over 50 cutting rooms working on every genre, with extensive post-production support, viewing theatres, transfer suites and dubbing theatres.

As an assistant editor with some worthwhile experience now under my belt I was working at one of the dynamic hubs of TV production on some interesting and prestigious programmes. These included *Birds Eye View*, which inter-weaved helicopter shots of the British Isles with diverse location items (a forerunner to *Coast*), and documentaries from the legendary portfolio of the BBC Adventure unit, headed by Bryan Branston, who despatched crews to far-flung corners of the world, most notably the Amazon Basin and rural North America, to further our understanding of anthropology. In simple terms this meant they set off in search of exotic plants, dormant volcanoes, cannibals and lost tribes, putting themselves in immense danger with every visit. These early pioneers would be gone for months on end, completely out of contact, without the benefit of mobile phones, satellite links, Sat-Navs, wi-fi or laptop computers, until they turned up one day at the studio gates with piles of film cans that needed processing so that they and the nation could relive the excitement of their adventures. Amazingly they all returned in one piece, nobody left behind with their head wedged inside an alligator's jaw or bubbling away inside a cooking pot.

The twelve months I spent at Ealing were extraordinary to say the least. It was a magnet for some of the most gifted and notable filmmakers working in television. And everyone who worked at the studios had ample opportunity to play a part in the production process. Sound engineers would sometimes waylay me on my way to lunch to help provide off-screen cries and death screams for battle scenes in the dubbing theatre, and assistant directors often purloined my services as a background walk-on for some exterior filming that was taking place on the lot.

Most excitingly, Ken Russell had been making his documentary-dramas for the BBC on composers for the *Monitor* series. *Elgar* and *The Debussy Film* had already made their mark and *Song of Summer*, on the life of Frederick Delius, was his latest offering before he headed off to make his cinematic masterpiece *Women in Love,* followed by *Tommy, The Music Lovers* and *Altered States.* Many regarded Russell as a flamboyant wacko, obsessed with sexuality and the

27

Catholic Church and out of control with his visualisations. To me he was a cinematic genius who has not been accorded the recognition he deserves for the role he played in the development of British film. Since his death in 2011 his ground-breaking *Monitor* films have neither been broadcast nor re-released as a tribute, including his film biopic of the dancer Isadora Duncan with its stunning visual interpretations. Ken Russell may have courted controversy during his lifetime but he was the one filmmaker who inspired me more than any other to want to become a director. He was, however, one charismatic programme-maker amongst a whole raft of talented producers and directors working for the BBC who took chances in pushing the creative boundaries and setting the bar for all who followed in their wake.

It was with great regret that I had to leave Ealing Studios when my contract with the BBC finally expired. There are few occupations where you can share a coffee and a sandwich with a band of surly cut-throat pirates one week, a unit of injured soldiers from the First World War trenches the next, and a horde of St Trinian's schoolgirls wielding hockey sticks the week after. It was like stepping into a Time Machine that had no affinity with the real world, but was enormous fun nevertheless. Time itself stood still for those twelve months, even though I knew it wouldn't last, and when I finally walked out of the studio gates I was destined not to return to these particular studios for thirty eight years.

Frustrating though it may be, freelancers in the unpredictable world of television have to shelve their disappointments, adapt to change and regard every move as a new challenge and opportunity. It was with this in mind that I took up employment as an assistant editor with Thames Television in the summer of 1969, hoping to find a way to edit programmes rather than just assist. Thames had won the licence to broadcast programmes for London and the surrounding counties for the ITV network the preceding year and their studios in Kingsway were excessively busy. I was assigned to the children's programme *Magpie*, which transmitted live, twice weekly, from the Kingsway studios and was promoted as ITV's trendy, accessible answer to the BBC's *Blue Peter*. It was produced by Sue Turner and presented by Tony Bastable, a former journalist and news reporter, Susan Stranks, a former child actress, and Radio 1 DJ Pete Brady. Each took turns to front magazine items for the show, some of which were filmed on location the previous week, others that took place live, in the studio, many of the items researched by one of the show's future presenters, Mick Robertson. *Magpie* claimed to have a large adult following, testament to the rich, varied and detailed items that were so professionally presented within such a tight timescale.

My immediate boss was Rosemary McGoughlin, an experienced film editor who could stand her ground with awesome effect. When Sue Turner introduced extra location items to the schedule, Rosemary's workload immediately increased and she championed me as an assembly editor to deal with the overflow. In a union-dominated environment this did not go down particularly well with the staff editors and assistants who, quite reasonably, didn't see why a newcomer - a freelance - should walk in off the streets and pinch a coveted job. But pinch it I did – and even though I was amazed that the ACTT had allowed it to happen, I decided it best to ignore the hoo-ha going on around me and busy myself editing location items, for which I received my first on-screen credit, sometimes observing studio sessions from the gallery during rehearsals and live transmissions.

Accidents on *Magpie* were a rarity during that glorious summer but there was the occasional disaster. Susan was thrown from a hot-air balloon basket during a location shoot and knocked unconscious and Pete Brady had a mishap with a cooking utensil inside a flammable tent. As for Tony, he had the misfortune to spend part of an afternoon watching a film with me - on the surface the safest of all three leisure pursuits. Our purpose was to select a scene from the 1955 film *Richard III* starring Laurence Olivier. Halfway through the screening, in a semi-darkened room, Tony put a cigarette in his mouth and I obliged by offering him a light from a lighter that had been warming up in my pocket all day. The dazzling flash of yellow that suddenly erupted from it shot to the ceiling like an industrial flame-thrower, emptying the entire contents in one sizzling blast, singeing both his eyebrows and forehead and forcing him to retreat to his dressing room for a complete make-over before he went live on air about an hour later. He was full of apologies for having leant over too far, not realising his card had been marked from the moment he sat down next to me. When Sue Turner saw the clip we had selected of the two young princes being locked in the tower she decided it was too frightening for younger viewers and the item was scrapped anyway.

My personal winter of discontent followed when the company transferred their entire London operation to a large complex in Euston and *Magpie* was moved to Teddington Studios, where it sadly incorporated fewer film inserts. Since this now made my job defunct, I reverted to my former role of assistant editor for the remainder of my contract, a little annoyed at having to take a backward step but with a need to stay in circulation and to keep earning. As I was to discover in the ensuing years, there are times when you have to bite the bullet and face-off disappointment and accept that as one door slams shut another swings open, in my case creating a series of unforgettable escapades and adventures.

For the moment it was business as usual. I was assigned to one of Thames TV's most highly regarded editors, Trevor Waite, who had just begun work on a documentary called *The Hardest Way Up* about the expedition to conquer the south face of Annapurna, which was being undertaken by some of the world's most experienced climbers, led by Chris Bonnington. It was a topical story, filmed and edited as the expedition progressed, under the watchful eyes of producer John Edwards and Executive Producer Jeremy Isaacs.

At 8091 metres, the summit of Annapurna is the tenth highest in the world. Although it was the first 8000-meter peak to be climbed, many consider it to be the hardest and is said to be the least frequently climbed 8000-metre peak, severe challenges facing the climbers at every turn. The footage was beautifully filmed, some of the most breath-taking scenes ever recorded, by one of the climbers, Mick Burke, as he swung across crevices hundreds of feet in the air, armed with pickaxe and crampons. I had enormous respect for the way he worked his way up the mountain enduring various extremes of temperatures, filming the ascent with meticulous care. When he returned to England after filming was completed, I took the opportunity to go with him down to Harrison's Crag to record sound effects that would replace the unwanted rustles and wind noises that had been recorded with the rushes. Understanding the important role that a soundtrack can play in the making of a film was an immense education and it was rewarding to see a finished film that blended the dangers of the climb seamlessly with the loneliness and isolation experienced by the mountaineers. The film was hugely successful but the realities of the dangers struck home a year or so later when Mick Burke was with a party that attempted to reach the summit of Mount Everest during deteriorating weather conditions but did not return. In his memory the BBC created the Mick Burke Award for filmmakers, jointly run by the BBC and the Royal Geographical Society, a fitting tribute to a man whose sense of humour, courage and talent will be remembered by many.

As my contract with Thames TV drew to a close, I braced myself for a period of general uncertainty as I looked for work in an increasingly crowded freelance market. I had hoped my brief experience working as an editor would stand me in reasonable contention but it wasn't enough to secure any long-term contracts. Since I didn't want to stay on the assistant treadmill for longer than was necessary, I began writing comedy sketches with a colleague, Dan Carter, and within a few weeks we were offered a short-term contract with ATV for *The Marty Feldman Comedy Machine* which was being produced by Larry Gelbart, the American writer/producer responsible for the smash hits *M*A*S*H* and *Tootsie*. I had met Marty only briefly a few years earlier when I worked on his documentary *One Pair of Eyes*, but when Dan and I paid a visit to Elstree Studios he remembered our sessions and invited us to view a rushes session with him. Halfway through the screening he put a cigarette in his mouth and asked if I had a light. I obligingly put my hand in my pocket, fumbled around for the warm lighter nestling inside it, thought better of it, and told him I had given up smoking. The last thing I needed at that pivotal point in my career was to set fire to the hugely popular Marty Feldman's hair.

Dan and I submitted sketches for several shows that year but we were only ever peripheral writers who were not part of the core writing teams and the contracts were always short-term agreements. Working ludicrous hours dreaming up comic one-liners that might never see the light of day seemed a waste of valuable resources so we decided to stick to what we did best, assuming suitable work would be forthcoming. Which it wasn't for two or three months.

Then, in the spring of 1971, came a call from Head of Film at Thames, John Zambardi, asking if I would be interested in joining a new unit based at Teddington Studios headed by Jeremy Isaacs. The series was to be called *The World at War*, rumoured to be one of the most ambitious - and expensive – undertaken in the history of documentary production, with narration by Laurence Olivier. The job on offer was dubbing editor, which involved the researching, recording and track-laying of sound effects, in some instances to entire battle scenes that had been shot mute during the countless wartime engagements. Working with Jeremy Isaacs and some of the most experienced documentary filmmakers in the country would be a tremendous experience, so I didn't need to think twice about joining the unit. It would not only secure me work for three years, but help hone the sound editing skills I had started to develop on *The Hardest Way Up*.

And so it was that a group of fifty of us set up camp at Teddington Studios on April 1st 1971, ready to take on one of the biggest challenges that television could embark on: twenty-six one hour episodes featuring prominent generals and politicians of every nationality, talking of their experiences alongside ordinary men and women who had endured seven long years of hardship and uncertainty. All edited together with archive footage researched in film libraries around the world; an unfolding saga of an extraordinary series of events in world history. And I was to be a part of it. As a bonus I also witnessed a prolific age of studio production at Teddington that saw the likes of Tommy Cooper, Benny Hill, Sid

James and Edward Woodward appearing regularly on the studio lot, with shows such as *Public Eye, Feel the Width, The Tomorrow People* and *Love Thy Neighbour* battling to be ratings winners in both drama and situation comedy. As if that wasn't enough, this abundance of talent came together in a picturesque part of Middlesex on a well-equipped production site situated next to the weir at Teddington Lock, complete with a hospitality boat, a bar and two restaurants that overlooked a beautiful stretch of the River Thames.

The studios themselves had a fascinating history, beginning with acquisition of the site in the 1880's by wealthy stockbroker Henry Chinnery, whose keen interest in cinematography led to him to allow a group of film enthusiasts to use his greenhouse as a studio during a rainstorm. A series of short comedy films were recorded on the grounds between 1912 and 1922, followed by numerous full-length features that were filmed in an enclosed sound stage, and in 1931, having been upgraded with the latest equipment, the property was renamed Teddington Film Studios. Warner Brothers took over the site in the same year and a variety of features were made there, Errol Flynn making his screen debut in the 1934 mystery crime thriller *Murder at Monte Carlo*, now listed as one of the British Film Institute's seventy-five 'most wanted' lost films. The war years saw two of the studios destroyed by a flying bomb but they were subsequently rebuilt and when ABC Television purchased the site in 1958 it was adapted for television production on a grand scale. In 1960 the studios began recording the hugely successful *The*

Avengers and at the end of the decade ABC Television merged with the London company Rediffusion to form Thames Television, producing over the next two decades an immeasurable number of television shows that gave the BBC a run for its money, many being sold internationally. When I arrived at Teddington Studios to start work on *The World at War* in 1971, I was to play a small but privileged role in a unique period in British television production; a dream scenario – although for me it was a dream that almost came crashing down one cold, infamous night in late October.

The build up to this unwelcome and farcical event began a few weeks earlier when I was scouring the UK sound libraries for suitable sound effects and going on location and recording those that were difficult to find. We had decided from the outset to make the soundtracks as realistic as possible, so rather than simply dub in general background battle sounds from the various sound libraries, we opted to layer the tracks so that each gun, rifle shot, footstep, swooping fighter jet, or passing jeep would have its own authentic sound mixed in. This involved a great deal of labour-intensive work as we sourced the correct sounds and then had the task of synching them to the visuals so that the viewing public would believe that picture and sound were filmed simultaneously. In truth, the majority of footage taken during the war was mute, which meant for any single episode I was faced with the prospect of bringing some forty minutes of battle to life by laying in sound effects that were both realistic and accurate. To this end the production manager, Liz Sutherland, had arranged for me to travel to Plymouth on a bitterly cold day to the naval training academy to record a variety of sound effects for a sequence involving the famous D-Day landing, which was to be re-enacted by a group of sea cadets. The navy had a couple of authentic flat-bottomed landing craft in Plymouth so I would be able to record realistic sounds of the vessels sweeping up onto the beach, followed by the clatter of troops disembarking and charging towards enemy positions. It all sounds a bit Monty Python but since it was only the soundtrack we would be using and not the visuals it seemed a fairly straightforward task. One drawback was that I had only passed my driving test a few weeks earlier and was lacking in any meaningful navigation skills, so I turned up at the academy an hour late, alarmed to find the sound recordist we had commandeered from Westward Television waiting in the freezing cold, along with thirty young lads dressed only in dark blue cadet jumpers and shorts. Their commanding officer obviously considered it unmanly for them to stand around wearing coats, scarves and gloves, but it made me feel immensely guilty and it took a good half an hour to get them warmed up, running relays up and down the shingle beach.

To motivate them I suggested they imagine the enemy was about to engage them in combat, but boys being boys they took this literally and several fights broke out, with the perpetrators having to be peeled apart before we could carry on. When we finally set off with them all huddled together in a landing craft, the sea had become unusually choppy. Whilst the sound recordist, a seasoned sailor, revelled in capturing the sounds of bow wave, spray, water crashing against the sides of the craft and the crunching of pebbles as we slid onto the beach, I spent a miserable time throwing up and wishing I was somewhere else. Nothing compared to what those courageous soldiers endured in June 1944, of course, when hundreds were cut down before they made it to the beach; many before they even hit the water. No practice run or re-enactment for them; their moment was immediate and forever as they swept in on a bloody river of dreadful circumstance to face the enemy. It must have been a living hell.

When I eventually called a wrap, the boys hurried back to the warmth of their base and I climbed back into my car feeling nauseas, tired and with very little feeling left in my fingers and toes and made my way back home, hoping it had all been worth it. Analysis of the tapes the next day revealed that the sound recordist had captured some excellent sound effects, many of which would be used extensively on several of the series episodes rather than just the one sequence they were originally intended for. A good day's work achieved with more than a modicum of luck.

A few weeks after my return from Plymouth, I had logged the precious sound effects and was working with Alan Afriat, who edited several programmes himself and was also the Supervising Editor. Alan had been Thames Television's senior editor long before I had joined the company and by reputation ran a tight ship. He was also my immediate boss. We had been working until about eight o'clock one evening preparing the tracks for a sound mix later that week, and were both pretty bushed by the time we stumbled out of the cutting room. It wasn't unusual for us to make early starts and late finishes in the race to meet deadlines. On one or two occasions I had gone to bed in a state of near exhaustion, dreaming dreams that were completely devoid of sound, only to return to the beginning of the dream to lay in the sound effects and music. Having a mindset where reality fused with fantasy in such a bizarre way was something I should probably have had checked out with a psychologist, but never found the time.

On this particular evening Alan had headed off home and I followed shortly after, but as I drove towards the main gate, one of the security guards suddenly ran out in front of me, gesticulating wildly in the direction of the production block.

'Do you know your cutting room's on fire?' he shouted.

'You're kidding!'

'I'm not kidding, son.'

'But that's not possible, I've only just left…'

'Well it's definitely your room, and it's on fire!'

I was dumbstruck, but I could tell he was serious. I turned the car round and headed back to the production area thinking there must be some mistake, but as I rounded the corner the scene that greeted me brought my eyes out on stalks. Smoke was billowing from the cutting room door, flames were leaping out of the windows, and a group of people were engaged in all kinds of frenzied activity, tossing film cans onto the ground and stomping on a variety of burning embers. How was it possible that the dark empty room I'd left less than three minutes beforehand could possibly be ablaze?

'Is this your room?' bellowed a voice by the side of me.

I looked round and my heart sank. It was the Site Supervisor, and he was livid.

'Yes, but…'

'What the hell do you think you're playing at?'

'But I didn't….'

'The whole studio could have gone up, you stupid sod! People could have been killed!'

I looked around for any sign of Alan or anyone else I could share the guilt with but I was the only member of the entire production unit left on site.

'Look I'm sorry, but I've absolutely no idea how this could have happened.'

'Well you're going to have some explaining to do, that I can promise you!'

It was as if I'd wandered into a Roman Polanski movie, filled with distorted images and shadowy figures, all giving me a hard time. The Head of Security, who had just finished beating some flames out in a rubbish bin, walked over and held it out to me.

'Are these yours?' he asked, pointing into the bin.

I peered inside. Nestling at the bottom, and remarkably untouched by the fire, were half a dozen cigarette ends. It was just my luck that even though the room had almost gone up like a tinderbox the incriminating evidence had somehow survived.

'Yes, they're mine,' I said, 'but the last time I had a cigarette was lunchtime.'

My air of innocence didn't fool him. He eyed me suspiciously and pulled out a sooty filter tip. 'These things can smoulder,' he said, turning it over in his fingers.

'Not for seven hours,' I suggested, 'What about the pipe tobacco?'

He looked intently deeper into the bin and I stared with him into the dark recess. 'Those curly bits. They could be from Alan's pipe.'

He dug his fingers in and pulled out some small brown strands.

'I'm not saying Alan's pipe started the fire, because it could just as easily have been a cigarette. Or an electrical fault.'

'Well whatever it was,' said the Site Supervisor, 'you're in big trouble. Make sure you're here first thing in the morning.'

It was all so surreal. I'd actually dropped my boss in the mire, and there was more chaos to come, because with everyone being so distracted by the fire, they had forgotten that *Opportunity Knocks* had finished recording in the main studio and an audience of about two hundred pensioners had poured out onto the tarmac and boarded four waiting coaches. As the coaches made their way up the drive in a procession, two fire engines came howling around the corner, the result being a momentary stand-off. The images of confusion and pandemonium that ensued as the coaches started reversing back and the fire engines edged forward is still etched in my memory. How it didn't make the evening news bulletins I shall never know, but it looked very much as if my time on *The*

World at War was about to come to a sudden and premature end.

The next morning, I drove down to the studios early to find Alan sitting inside his cutting room looking somewhat perturbed and in earnest conversation with Peter Lee Thompson, one of the other editors. Alan had left the room in one piece the night before but this morning it was all charred and smoky, with black film cans sitting where there used to be nice shiny silver ones.

'We had a fire last night,' I said, stating the blatantly obvious, 'which started in the rubbish bin according to security. A cigarette. Or a pipe.'

All three of us glanced down at Alan's pipe, which was emitting small wisps of smoke, and he stubbed it out with his thumb. He had already inspected the inside of the cans and by some miracle the film rolls were all okay but the real problem was going to be explaining the whole thing away to Liz Sutherland, Jeremy and Thames TV security. We had, after all, accumulated a vast amount of irreplaceable film in the adjacent production block and the ramifications of losing it all in one fell swoop just didn't bear thinking about. My personal embarrassment intensified when the Head of Security called by later that morning to begin the inquest.

He updated Alan on the events of the preceding night, leading to the conclusion that it was either a cigarette or a pipe that was the culprit.

'Mr Harvey, you don't believe it was a cigarette, do you?'

I gave Alan a sideways glance. 'Well, I didn't say that exactly. My last recollection of having a cigarette was about lunchtime, although it could have been mid-afternoon. I don't recall it being near to going home time'.

He looked at me long and hard, like I was a fish wriggling on a hook, but didn't pursue it, mainly because Alan admitted it was possible his pipe was to blame, since he did tap the ash into the bin occasionally. The conversation went around in circles for a while, before they both left, having drawn no firm conclusions as to exactly what happened. We didn't hear very much after that, except for the appearance of NO SMOKING signs in all the rooms a day or so later and I thought that at the very least we would be carpeted by the management.

Curiously, nothing more was ever said, and although it was true that the whole thing had been an accident, I suspect Jeremy had a hand in keeping a lid on the saga. All of us had been under intense pressure for some time and Jeremy knew we were working hours well beyond the call of duty. Apart from that, he had a reputation for being loyal to his production staff, which was one of the many reasons he commanded such respect. He had a flair for making the right editorial decisions and motivating people to give of their best.

Whilst the incident had no immediate fall-out I was transferred to cutting rooms at Twickenham Film Studios for a few months - not, I was assured, because I was a potential danger to myself and the production unit as a whole but because Twickenham studios had an extensive sound library and excellent sound transfer facilities, which they did. The technicians on site offered a fast and high quality turnaround as our transmission days drew ever closer and the pressure to finish on schedule began to build. It was also great fun working at a film studio where the likes of Richard Lester, Richard Attenborough and Ridley Scott made many of their landmark movies such as *Help! Blade Runner, A Fish Called Wanda, Cry Freedom, Shadowlands,* and *Superman,* alongside the majority of the world's most renowned producers and directors. My cutting room was sandwiched between the Monty Python team and their editing crew working on *Monty Python and the Holy Grail* and *The Day of the Locusts*, a feature film directed by John Schlesinger and edited by the incomparable Jim Clark. Schlesinger was an English theatre and film director who had won an Academy Award for *Midnight Cowboy* in 1969 and made some of the most outstanding films of the sixties and seventies, including *Billy Liar, Far from the Madding Crowd, Marathon Man* and *Darling*. Because I was the only editor on site working on the smaller gauge 16mm as opposed to 35mm, I was privileged to have him call in occasionally to view some reels of 16mm film he was using for his lecture tours. He was a charming man with a wealth of stories and an abundance of talent that only a select group of cinema directors can lay claim to and his legacy is one of the greatest gifts the industry has been left with.

I also occasionally bumped into Vic Gallucci, an old friend who had worked for some years as a projectionist at Twickenham Odeon but now made his living as a film extra, wandering around the lot in various guises, from an Arab sheik one day, to a fireman, or a pirate, the next. Vic was also listed in the Guinness Book of Records as the longest serving extra in a TV Show, playing DC Baker in *The Bill.* In the seventies Twickenham Film Studios saw a veritable cascade of movies pass through its doors. In later years it was to go into administration and was destined for demolition until the 'Save Twickenham Studios' campaign was formed, drawing attention to the imminent loss of a vital piece of film history. The campaign was successful and the site was purchased by property magnate Sunny Vohra, who not only reopened the complex but completely modernised and re-equipped it. One of my fondest memories of working at the studios was attending a Christmas party held in the main sound stage. A glittering array of producers, directors and actors rolled up for the grand evening bash, chatting excitedly among the Egyptian pillars and statues that had been borrowed from the props store to add an air of eastern mystique to the proceedings. As the evening wore on the ornate columns and sculptures began to topple and fall apart, unable to sustain their dignity and stand upright as they were continually pushed and jostled by the intoxicated gathering. The sound stage looked as if it had been hit by an earthquake by the time everybody left, though I doubt if anyone noticed. As for me, Christmas that year offered little respite from the pressing needs of the series as there was still much work to be done and by the time we slipped into the New Year, dubbing sessions had been scheduled and the task of mixing the various soundtracks was upon us.

Once mixed, the music and voice-overs were added, including the twenty-six programme commentaries read by Laurence Olivier. When I attended the first Olivier voice recording session for *France Falls* in a sound studio just off Oxford Street, the reading did not go particularly well. Jeremy had asked Olivier to give an understated performance that would contrast with the excitement and passion of the participants' voices and the drama and noise of war. It was a positive creative approach but Olivier's narration did not fulfil Jeremy's expectations. When the session was over there was concern that Olivier, acknowledged as the world's greatest actor, would have to do it again or be replaced, an outcome that nobody wanted. Jeremy was determined to make it work. He arranged to play the programme back to Olivier, who himself conceded that it wasn't good enough. He re-recorded his soundtrack but a few days later announced that he wanted to pull out. He had recently completed sixteen weeks of filming on *Sleuth* and been performing the demanding play *Long Day's Journey into Night* for three weeks on the London stage and was known to have been ill. He was, not surprisingly, tired, his fatigue reflected in his narration. Jeremy recalls going to see Olivier's agent and being asked if he had told Olivier how wonderful he was. It hadn't seemed necessary to offer such reassurance but even the revered Olivier, it seemed, needed encouragement and praise.

Fortunately, Olivier agreed to continue, though I did not attend any more voice recording sessions after that first one. Jeremy kept the attendees to a minimum, making sure that Olivier was relaxed and in good spirits as soon as he turned up, watching each film with him before the recordings, working with him to ensure that each reading was delivered with subtlety and strength, but compelling rather than flowery – and the results were, in all twenty-six episodes, sublime and as near to perfection as anyone could hope for.

But Olivier was not the only artist of stature who gave added authenticity to the series. Carl Davis's extraordinary music score remains both inspirational and haunting. Carl's early work in the USA provided valuable conducting experience with organisations such as the New York City Opera. In 1959 the revue *Diversions*, of which he was co-author, won an off-Broadway Emmy and the show subsequently travelled to the Edinburgh Festival in 1961. As a direct result of its success there, Davis was commissioned by Ned Sherrin to compose music for the original British version of the TV series *That Was the Week That Was*. He achieved early prominence with the title music for the BBC's anthology drama series *The Wednesday Play* and later for *Play for Today* and other television scores include *The Naked Civil Servant, The Hound of the Baskervilles, The Far Pavilions and Pride and Prejudice.* He also scored a number of films, including *The French Lieutenant's Woman* (for which he won the BAFTA Award for Best Film Music), *Champions, The Great Gatsby, Mothers & Daughters* and *The Understudy*.

Two of his finest and most memorable television works were for *Unknown Chaplin* and the *Hollywood* series which told the story of the early days of the silent film, made for Thames Television in 1980 and narrated by James Mason. The fabulously seductive opening title sequence, edited by Trevor Waite and scored by Carl, is a master class in how to secure the viewer's interest before the main programme has begun. For me, however, his extraordinary score for *The World at War* will always be his finest achievement, not simply because the canvas he had to work on was so vast, but because his blending of pathos, tragedy and humour help the viewer become totally absorbed in stories of enormous complexity whilst sustaining complete emotional involvement.

It is no accident that *The World at War* has since been acclaimed as one of the finest documentary series ever made, winning a stack of coveted awards, including a Bafta and an Emmy, and has been sold to over a hundred countries, hardly ever having been off air in the forty-five years since it was made.

But *The World at War* was more than just a triumph of technical achievement. I discovered in my three years of viewing countless hours of library footage just what human beings are capable of; how some could inflict the utmost cruelty and suffering, how others endured the kind of hardship and loss that most of us could never contemplate and hope never to experience. Their stories have given the world a television series that records, unflinchingly, a terrible period in human history that should stand as a lesson for all time.

I did not return to Teddington Studios for twenty-three years, but the world-wide reputation of this one remarkable series created opportunities that I would never have believed possible and along the way opened my eyes to the extraordinary lengths that people will go to in order to secure recognition and achieve fulfilment in the unpredictable world of broadcast television.

THE FREELANCE TRAIL

I rode on the wave of *The World at War's* success for several months, working at many of the ITV regions as a freelance editor in cutting rooms where I had previously only been offered work as an assistant; most notably HTV in Bristol, Anglia Television in Norwich and Westward Television in Plymouth. I was not assigned to anything particularly ground-breaking or interesting, mostly news and current affairs, but it was important to expand the CV at every opportunity. Surprisingly, the nightly news programmes turned out to be more of a hassle than I had imagined, primarily because many of the items I had been editing during the day were replaced at the last minute when something deemed more important cropped up. Burst water mains or the opening of a new library by a local councillor - virtually anything regarded as exciting by the news editor - would instantly, and with little warning, replace other stories that we had been feverishly piecing together for transmission, such as a report on a surge in local carrot production.

I could never quite fathom why some reports were given priority over others. An impromptu visit to the studios by a celebrity or member of the Royal Family, for instance, would not only relegate stories of villagers fending off floodwaters, or barns catching fire, to the cutting room floor, but provide enough material to take over the entire evening's broadcast as well as being recycled for several weeks after. Rumour had it that when the Queen visited Norwich and the story was transmitted upside down in error, all hell broke loose and the offenders were unceremoniously hauled over the coals. The regional journalists didn't make the editors' lives any easier either, often leaving us twiddling our thumbs all day then delivering filmed rushes to the cutting room that were due to air within an hour or less. I had several close calls racing down corridors with edited stories that only just made it to transmission. I remember on one occasion working all day on a hugely entertaining three-minute story for Thames Television's *Today* programme featuring a Brazilian carnival troupe giving a vibrant street performance in Covent Garden. By ten minutes to six all my painstaking work began to unravel as the producer, who was in walkie-talkie contact with the studio gallery, hacked it down to a mere thirty seconds to make room for a mind-numbing political story that someone had considered far more interesting and relevant than my uplifting mini masterpiece. With the majority of local news programmes featuring such generally uninspiring items as sheep dog trials and cake-baking contests, it was little wonder that programme editors hoped and prayed for news of a local murder or an approaching tornado to liven up their day.

I was diligent in my efforts to avoid upsetting staff members with my outspoken views on union activity and company politics, or being the catalyst for anything that might dent my progress up the career ladder. Freelancers taking up employment at regional companies in the seventies faced a monumental wall of indifference, most of us regarded by the staff technicians as outsiders whose objective was to infiltrate the system and take their jobs. I had no such desire since my own ambitions lay elsewhere and I was perfectly happy to slide in and out of regional television employment without any commitment to long-term servitude or becoming part of any political back-biting, whilst making the most of local hospitality and spending some extremely enjoyable nights on the town, all expenses paid.

Farming Diary kept me busy in Norwich, with regular stints up to one in the morning to ensure we made transmission deadlines; *Report West* in Bristol offered one memorable evening of adrenaline-pumping excitement when an IRA bomb exploded in Park Street, turning the nightly news schedules on their head. And in Plymouth... well, Plymouth was another story altogether. A documentary on the life of the renowned stripper Fiona Richmond, *The Actress and the Bishop*, was being edited in one of the Westward TV cutting rooms and had already ruffled feathers throughout the network, even though its erotic content was frankly no match for the racy get-togethers being organised by some of the staff when they weren't busy working on their boats. Swinging seemed to have arrived in parts of the West Country long before it became widespread in the major cities, and my education in sexual high jinks took a sharp upward turn during my time at Westward. All in all an illuminating time; a great deal of fun and some worthwhile experiences along the way. But it was never going to do me any career favours and after a year or so my escalator ride had turned into a treadmill and I needed to have another serious rethink.

An escape route presented itself in the shape of *Candid Camera*, a hidden camera show that had proved popular in the early sixties and was about to make its comeback ten years later. *Candid Camera* had begun life as *Candid Microphone*, a series created by the American Allen Funt for radio broadcast in 1948, using hidden microphones to catch unsuspecting people worldwide in the spirit of fun. Following the success of *Candid Microphone*, *Candid Camera* was launched for television in the States in 1949 and became a top-rated TV show in both network runs and syndication, featuring among its writers and presenters, Woody Allen and Buster Keaton. British practical joker Jonathan Routh presented his own version of *Candid Mike* for Radio Luxembourg in 1957, made in association with Allen Funt, and distributed on Pye Records. Stunts included taking a piano for a ride on the Tube and Routh posting himself, covered in stamps, to Wandsworth.

In 1960 *Candid Camera* was launched by ABC Television in the UK, with Routh and Arthur Atkins as the practical jokers and the show was presented by British comedian Bob Monkhouse. The series ran between 1960 and 1967, during which Routh received a black eye from a disgruntled customer who was upset at being sold two left-handed teacups instead of two right-handed ones. Regretfully there were legal complications with the series generally and it ended its run until the English producer Peter Dulay acquired the European rights to the title from Funt and re-launched the series in 1974, without Routh, but featuring Arthur Atkins and Peter performing many of the stunts himself. This revised *Candid Camera*, made for London Weekend Television under the watchful eye of Programme Controller Michael Grade, attracted an audience of 7.1 million viewers, when the top-rated programme *This Is Your Life* was achieving a marginally higher 8.5 million.

Peter was a former comic who wrote comedy scripts for other performers, including the Copenhagen comedian and pianist Victor Borge, who worked frequently in England from 1956. Peter broke into television writing in 1961, co-scripting *Roamin' Holiday* with Eric Sykes as a vehicle for Max Bygraves, followed by contracts as a comedy writer in independent television. Among the many series he produced for ABC-TV were *Comedy Bandbox* (1962), a showcase for new comedians, including Hope and Keen, and *Frankie and Bruce* (1966), which co-starred two comedians surnamed Howerd and Forsyth. In 1969 he moved to Yorkshire Television for a long run as writer/producer of *Sez Les*, starring Les Dawson. Peter also managed artists such as Keith Harris and Larry Grayson, in between producing *The Tommy Cooper Show* and *Opportunity Knocks*. His father, Benson Dulay, had been a renowned magician in the twenties, so Peter's understanding of prop-making combined with comic timing made him the perfect presenter for *Candid Camera*. It was sheer luck that whilst I was looking for work, Peter was looking for a film editor who had worked in comedy. The Marty Feldman connection paid off in a way I had not expected and led to a long association with Peter and the *Candid Camera* franchise, starting with the second series in the summer of 1974, based at Twickenham Film Studios under the watchful eye of producer Kevin Bishop, who was later to direct many top entertainment shows for the BBC, including *Wogan, The Royal Variety Show* and *French and Saunders*. It featured a cavalcade of visual tomfoolery, from donuts flying off the end of an out-of-control conveyer belt as a perplexed operative tried to stop them, to skittles exploding on impact in a bowling alley, and a woman answering telephone calls about a new energy efficient 'smokeless stove' that poured an endless stream of smoke into the room, engulfing her in a thick smog, the design and execution of the props provided by the ever resourceful John Landon.

Following the success of the first two series, Michael Grade commissioned a further thirteen episodes, this time with the inclusion of Jonathan Routh. Routh complemented the regular team perfectly, lending his own brand of surrealist humour, from a birdman 'landing' on Wimbledon Common and persuading onlookers to give him a tow to get him airborne again, to a waiter distracting customers as a thirsty tulip drank from their teacups. Most of the fun was being had out on the road, of course, away from the confines of the cutting room, where I worked my way through several hours of material, sifting out the comic gems that would end up in the final shows.

Whilst Peter had done everything possible to ensure that the set pieces worked effectively, he was still reliant on the comic timings of the on-screen team, the props, and the general public playing their innocent part in the subterfuge. This meant that whole hours might pass by before the right mark stepped into shot and the stunt worked with the necessary precision.

For Peter, this meant filming enough material to put into thirteen half-hour shows without blowing the budget on film stock and processing. Back in 1974 there was no digital photography, no cost-effective tapes or camera cards to record onto, no miniature cameras that could be concealed invisibly inside rooms, no real-time viewing of set pieces, location sound having to be picked up by the operatives themselves or by microphones hidden inside vases, and no instant playback to check that everything was okay. And the more stunts the production team filmed that could not be used, the more costly and time consuming it all became. For cameraman Mike Fox and his crew, long days had to be spent concealed behind a camera hide that was built into suitable but confined areas of premises such as dry cleaners and travel agents, often next to the toilets, or crammed inside a camera van filming through one of the windows. Spending long hours cooped up in a metal box in temperatures of thirty-five degrees was not the most comfortable – or memorable – experience and everyone just prayed that they would be rewarded with stunts that were uproariously funny.

Fortunately, there was an ample supply of the gullible and the confused who wandered into unsuspecting situations and took the bait offered to them by Jonathan, Arthur Atkins, Shelia Burnette, Ken Wilson and Peter, and the results are a testament to their quick-thinking in unpredictable situations, along with their finely tuned comic abilities. Many shows have attempted to emulate the success of *Candid Camera* but few have mastered the skills required to make hidden camera comedy work at its best, the most basic being that the general public, caught on camera, have to be coerced into performing rather than members of the production team. In the majority of copycat hidden camera shows, actors or presenters give an on-screen performance that elicits little more than embarrassed laughter from the public, who don't actually do anything, so there is no meaningful contribution or interaction. This form of hidden camera filming involves little technique on the part of the actors and at best is lazy in its execution. One of the best examples from the *Candid Camera* archive I can use to illustrate this point involves Arthur Atkins and Sheila Burnette in *Arthur's Alibi*. This scenario takes place in a dry cleaners, where an unsuspecting member of the public, a dustman, has called in to collect his cleaning. Whilst engaged in conversation with Arthur, Arthur's wife (Sheila Burnette) calls in and asks her husband where he spent the night. Arthur immediately turns from Sheila to the dustman, saying 'I was with Mr Smith all night, wasn't I, Mr Smith?' The dustman, realising that Arthur is talking to him and is in need of an alibi, confirms that he had spent the night with him, even though he has never seen Arthur before in his life. The premise for this stunt is simple but requires excellent comic timing from the actors in order to gain maximum value from the dustman, who has unwittingly found himself in a less than desirable situation. The technique required for such a situation is to allow the mark (the dustman) to run with the deception, even though he is clearly uncomfortable with the fabrication, and for the actors to become observers and *not* performers as 'Mr Smith,' relates to Sheila details of the night's bonding session he has had with Arthur. At one point Arthur even exits the shop temporarily and the dustman takes off on a prolonged flight of fancy recalling their fictitious night out, inventing all manner of scenarios in order to put Sheila's mind at rest. It is a classic stunt that works because both Arthur and Sheila understood the psychology of the situation and how to allow the dustman to perform rather than themselves. If any members of Peter's team indulged in such egocentric routines they would get an ear-bashing they were not likely to forget. There were times, however, when I did think even Peter was pushing his luck.

One evening after a late night rushes viewing session I asked him what stunt he had planned for the next day. His eyes lit up immediately. 'We've rented an office in Richmond,' he said, his face infused with mischief, 'which for our purposes is a registry office. Jonathan plays the registrar and Ken Wilson and Eve Adam play the bride and groom.' He could hardly contain his excitement. 'Then we bring in a male passer-by from the street to act as a witness – and we marry him to the bride!' He chuckled his trademark chuckle, hardly able to contain himself. I responded with a respectful 'sounds terrific, Peter,' thinking it was an idea almost certainly bound for failure; a ruse that would never work in a million years. Which meant an entire day of filming would be wasted.

The following evening, I sat and watched the rushes of *The Wedding*, open-mouthed at the unfolding saga. A local milkman, who had been lured away from his milk float to be a witness, entered the room and announced his name as Mr Badcock to the registrar's assistant. I turned to Peter with obvious suspicion and he shrugged his shoulders. 'I know. Nobody will believe I didn't set this up.' It was not the last time I would hear those words. Unfortunately, every time the name Badcock was mentioned on camera it created a serious possibility for corpsing as Ken, Eve and Jonathan struggled to keep straight faces.

Mr Badcock went through his entire wedding vows, even kissing his new 'bride' as the stunt concluded. When Jonathan announced he was off to his next appointment and wished the happy couple well for the future, Mr Badcock's face crumpled into momentary panic and he protested that there must have been a misunderstanding and that he was already married. Jonathan responded with one of the best one-liners you're likely to hear in the history of hidden camera filming: 'But Mr Badcock, this is bigamy.'

It wasn't all fun and games making *Candid Camera*, however, and my own brush with near disaster came in Dublin several years later during the making of *The Candid Camera Connection* for RTE, which I co-directed with Peter and was, for the first time, recorded on videotape rather than film. The first week passed without incident, save for an unfortunate episode involving Ken Wilson picking Peter's pocket at a bus-stop, neither aware that the member of the public they were attempting to ensnare was an off-duty policeman. But this was only a preamble to the unwanted surprise we were given during the second week.

We had parked the camera van on the pavement outside a street café where two burly men were deep in conversation whilst drinking afternoon tea. Peter walked up to their table, sat in an empty chair opposite them, produced a packet of biscuits, and proceeded to dunk the biscuits in their tea. The men took the situation in their stride, not the least bit phased by the intrusion – until Peter revealed that they were being filmed by a hidden camera.

At this point the two men went berserk, one of them throwing the crockery from the table in a rage, the other hurling his chair into the air before they headed towards the van in blind fury. What followed was a terrifying few moments as we tried to placate them. I offered to erase the sequence from the tape, but it wasn't good enough; we either gave them the tape or serious injury was going to be inflicted and these guys were not kidding. The more I tried to reason with them, the angrier they became, until finally, with my body pinned up against the van door with a fist in my face, I instructed the cameraman to hand over the tape. It was with huge relief that we watched them walk off down the street, even though they were carrying an entire morning's fruitful and irretrievable filming in their hands.

I have no idea what the two men were planning at the café that day, but I have no doubt it involved sinister and violent criminal activity, such was their desperation to secure the evidence. One thing I do know is that we would have had our faces permanently disfigured if I had not complied and at the end of the day nothing is worth putting a crew at risk. I decided it might be wise to call a wrap at this location since, even without the tape, we could identify the men if called upon - a thought that would certainly occur to our assailants before too long. When the crew suggested we made a quick getaway, I didn't need any persuading. That said, situations that were liable to cause upset or offence were rare during the making of the series, the only time *Candid Camera* risked clashing with public opinion being when Allen Funt made a hilarious spin-off feature for the cinema in 1970 entitled *What Do You Say To a Naked Lady?* The film featured, among many risqué set-ups, naked secretaries stepping into offices to take notes armed with only a pen and notebook. Peter attempted a UK version but it seems audiences in the seventies were not prepared for such outrageous behaviour. One can only wonder if the same scenario, filmed today in offices and sex boutiques, featuring both men and women, would attract a more appreciative audience.

When *Candid Camera* departed from our screens in 1974, Peter was contracted as a hidden camera adviser on programmes such as the UK's *Late Late Breakfast Show*, presented by Noel Edmunds, along with numerous shows in Europe, including *Banana*

Split, a series he made with Ralph Inbar for TROS, Holland. I learned a great deal from him during our twenty-five year association, not just about the mechanics and politics of TV production but also the theatre, often attending productions that featured many of the artistes he represented, at venues as diverse as The London Palladium and Wimbledon Theatre. We even filmed some hidden camera film clips for inclusion in *The Black and White Minstrel Show* at the Winter Gardens, Weston-Super-Mare, a stage show based on a format that had been the mainstay of television entertainment at the BBC between 1958 and 1978. The Minstrel show presented traditional American minstrel and country songs, as well as show and music hall numbers performed in blackface and with lavish costumes, but despite its popularity – attracting viewing figures of 21 million by 1964 and picking up a Bafta in 1969 – it was axed by the BBC, rather belatedly, in 1978 due to its racial undertones. It continued touring provincial theatres, however, until 1987. The Weston-Super-Mare production featured the comedian Lenny Henry, full of high-octane energy and ambition, and ventriloquist Keith Harris, whose act he had devised with Peter and featured Orville the Duck who was covered in feathers but couldn't fly. Lenny went on to become a fine actor, appearing in TV dramas and Shakespeare plays on the London stage and received a knighthood in 2015 for his charity work for *Comic Relief.* Keith was a family performer in the seventies and although his popularity waned for a short while, he successfully reinvented himself in later years, spicing up his act with adult humour with a show called *Duck*

Off and appearing in documentaries, commercials and pop promos in which he astutely took the rise out of himself and his puppet companions. Keith first came to my attention when he made a guest appearance on *Candid Camera*, making the animals appear to talk at Bristol Zoo as onlookers looked on in astonishment. We met up again a couple of years later in Weston-Super-Mare, when I filmed several sequences with him for inclusion in the stage show. One evening at supper we heard a telephone ringing from somewhere on the table. Keith smiled, picked up a banana and conducted a conversation, including the voice at the other end of the imaginary line, to the amusement of the production crew and customers.

Peter's armoury of performers and agents read like a Who's Who of the entertainment world and he was able to assemble an array of talent at the drop of a hat, often giving work to pals who had fallen on hard times. I recall standing next to him in the wings of one of a London theatre one night, watching an old-time performer in the autumn of his career, riding a unicycle with a stick balanced on the end of his nose, on top of which were sat a cup, a saucer, a cup, a saucer and another cup. As he wobbled his bike around the stage, he randomly tossed sugar cubes into the air, catching them in the top cup.

'That's amazing,' I said to Peter, suitably impressed.

'That's nothing,' he replied, 'he used to use Demerara.'

When Peter died in 1999 it was, for me, very much the end of an era. He was one of the last of a special breed of writer/performers who had worked their way up in Music Hall and Variety and spent many years perfecting their craft. I owe him more than I could ever repay and the years that I was privileged to spend in his company will always be special.

JUMPING SHIP

By the mid-seventies, I had more or less exhausted my circuit of the ITV companies and felt it was time to get my feet back under the table at the BBC, where there was a possibility that more meaningful creative pursuit might be achieved. There had been growing animosity between ITV and the ACTT, including a stand-off that became a turning point in television drama production. It began when George Taylor, Head of Film at Thames TV, and Lloyd Shirley, Head of Drama, set up a subsidiary company called Euston Films, with the specific aim of making gritty, grass roots detective dramas. The ACTT objected to the fact that Euston Films was using a school in Hammersmith, West London, to double as a police station for *Special Branch,* with the entire series being filmed on location rather than using one of the many available sound stages.

Up to this point sound stages had always been the sensible option for producers making dramas. The lighting and continuity is more controllable, filming can continue despite changing weather conditions, and the sound is recorded without interference from street noise, aeroplanes or the general public taking too close an interest in proceedings. Using sound stages for the majority of drama and entertainment programmes therefore has tremendous advantages but if you are on a tight budget studio hire can be expensive when you factor in office facilities, on-site prop-builders, set designers chippies and gaffers. When Euston Films rejected this traditional route in favour of on-location filming - known as four-wallers - the union attempted to block production. They overlooked the fact that if companies like Euston Films could not afford costly studio facilities, they were left with only two options: not to make the series at all or to be unrealistically economical with their budgets. Whilst location filming meant fast turnarounds, using lightweight crews and lightweight equipment, it happened to suit series like *Special Branch* in terms of its all-important in-your-face graphic realism.

The result was that several hundred writers, directors and technicians, including myself, marched around Soho Square carrying banners and chanting our disapproval; the first and only time I would be seen engaged in such rebellious activity – but it was important that precedents would not be set that would place any number of future productions into unwanted and inappropriate straight-jackets. To give him his due, Alan Sapper emerged after half an hour to address the angry crowd, with the opening words: 'Welcome to Soho Square.' We got the point. If more of us took an active part in union matters it would ensure a more balanced representation of opinion. Which is never easy when you are focused on doing your job and you know that union matters will eat into your time. Fair enough, but the Euston Films conundrum came down to everyone being realistic about the available options, and that meant giving producers freedom of choice, both financially and creatively.

In the end the ACTT relented, Euston Films made *Special Branch* as a four-waller, followed by *The Sweeney* and the immensely popular *Minder,* neither of which would have seen the light of day if a bunch of us had not got up off our backsides and participated in a pivotal moment in broadcasting history. It did little to avert an ongoing series of clashes the technicians had with ITV management, however, resulting in the longest, costliest and bitterest dispute in broadcast television, when, in 1979, the entire ITV network was shut down for more than ten weeks. Fortunately, I had managed to switch allegiance to the BBC some weeks before, even though I hadn't worked for the Corporation for almost a decade, but my accumulated experience on *The World at War* and at the many regional ITV stations created an opportunity to prise open a few doors. Dave Zeigler, a Films Operation Manager at Lime Grove, remembered me from my days at Radius Films with Stan Hawkes and Arthur Solomon and was encouraged enough by my CV to offer a contract on the *Songs of Praise* series, which was in need of an editor; fortunately not an editor of shining virtue who was in search of redemption or spiritual cleansing, or who had experienced a recent epiphany; just a technician of shameless ambition who was in need of a job for a few weeks.

I promptly hired myself a cutting room in Shepherd's Bush, delighted to be recognised as a professional editor contracted to a BBC TV series that had a large following. *Songs of Praise* may not float everyone's boat, but for me it was the perfect vehicle to hone my technical skills since it combined music coverage filmed on three cameras, interwoven with single camera documentary segments, all of which had to be edited seamlessly to create half an hour of informative entertainment. Fortunately, the Producer/Director Andrew Barr was very proficient in filming the variety of shots I needed in order to make it all work and the six months we spent working together were supremely rewarding.

Cultivating strong working relationships is a pre-requisite for success in any business and in television accumulated technical knowledge alone is never enough. Teamwork and trust go a long way towards creating engaging shows and Andrew and I made some terrific programmes together. One of the most memorable was the story of the Christmas truce of 1914, when candles and paper lanterns appeared on enemy parapets on the Western Front and soldiers from both sides sang carols. On Christmas Day they took part in a game of football in the snow, after which they returned to their positions in the trenches and resumed firing at one another. The hundredth anniversary of the start of World War One was recognised in 2014 with a raft of documentaries and dramas illustrating the horrors of that dreadful war, but back in 1977 Andrew Barr had tracked down some of these First World War veterans, all in their mid-eighties, and their vivid eye-witness accounts of The Christmas Truce gave an extraordinary insight into this historic event. Many of the shows in the *Songs of Praise* series, in fact, featured ordinary people who had amazing stories to tell, each offering enlightenment and inspiration, making me realise just how wonderful human beings can be under the most trying and difficult of circumstances.

Although it was an enjoyable experience, my itchy feet were soon telling me it was time to move on again and I told Andrew I felt compelled to explore other possibilities in an effort to increase the credibility of my portfolio. He was sorry I had made the decision to step down - especially as a financially attractive six-month contract on the series was in the offing – but he understood my reasons. We had a parting drink one evening, said our goodbyes, and I assumed that would be that.

A week later I received a call from Ken Cooper, another operations manager working at Lime Grove, who told me Andrew had been enthusing about my work to him and would I be interested in editing a one hour *Tonight* special to commemorate the anniversary of the assassination of Martin Luther King? I whooped quietly to myself and told him I'd very much like to work on the programme, particularly as the producer was the highly respected Jack Saltman. I hired the same cutting room, along with an assistant editor, but when I started work on the project a week later, little did I realise that a near calamity would almost stop my BBC career dead in its tracks - if it hadn't also turned out to be my saving grace.

The first two weeks of editing went well – better than I could have hoped - and Jack was delighted with the way the programme was shaping up. Piecing together countless vox-pop interviews, archive footage and newly filmed sequences that would reflect a fair balance of opinion took long days and nights and we were both worn out by the time the film was completed. To understand what happened next requires a brief note of technical explanation because film, unlike video, does not create an immediate transmittable end product. Today, all recorded video rushes are computerised and either held on a hard drive until needed, or edited instantly and broadcast without any delay. In the seventies film had to jump over several hurdles. At the initial film rushes stage a print was struck from the negative that was then edited as a rough cutting-copy which, over a period of time, accumulated a variety of scratches, rips and tears during repeated viewing sessions. When the editing was complete, this cutting copy was sent with the original, untouched, virgin negative to a neg-cutter who reassembled the film by matching embedded key numbers so that a brand new, perfect quality print could be produced by the film laboratory ready for transmission. And so, on 20th April 1979, four days before the programme's scheduled terrestrial transmission, I packaged up the original negatives and despatched them with the cutting copy, via a London cabbie, to the neg-cutters, secure in the knowledge that we would make transmission with a good three days to spare.

Except that when I turned up for work the next day I found Jack and Ken Cooper standing in the cutting room looking grim faced. The neg-cutters, who should have completed the neg-cut overnight, had rung in to say that they had received the negative but not the cutting copy and had therefore been unable to complete the final assembly. I was mortified. It was impossible. I had handed everything

70

over to the cabbie and he definitely had all the vital components inside his cab when he left the cutting room. But it was his word against mine and unless the cutting copy resurfaced very quickly, we were well and truly stuffed. The BBC attempted a somewhat lame, if not farcical, re-enactment later that morning in which the same cab driver turned up at the cutting room and was given a fake pile of cans to deliver to the neg-cutters, in the hope that memories might be jogged. But they were not. If the cutting copy had slid down the side of the seat and been discovered by a curious, possibly drunk, and not altogether honest passenger, the likelihood of us ever seeing it again was slender to say the least.

The question now was whether there was any way we could still make the transmission date. I was desperate to find a solution because the possibility of being fired from a BBC cannon on my first ever network documentary loomed large on the horizon. Already there was talk of cancelling the broadcast and I could see my career starting to unravel. 'If we can reprint all the rushes I think I can piece them together again from memory,' I suggested. Jack and Ken were not convinced. Even if that were possible it would take days, if not weeks, added to which all the soundtracks had now been split into different sections ready for sound mixing. They discounted the idea, thinking I was either clutching at straws or had taken leave of my senses. With film running at twenty-five frames per second, it meant that any one scene only had to be two frames adrift to look out of synch. There were well over a hundred edits in our programme and every cut point had to be precise to the frame in order to match the now disembodied soundtrack but I had enough experience to know that a film's template can stay fixed in an editor's mind for several days after completion and felt reasonably confident that I could make an exact replica. 'I know it sounds crazy, but we still have the sound sections running to length, and I know every edit instinctively, so I think it is possible.'

Despite their misgivings, they knew that either I attempted the unlikely or they cancelled the transmission, so a reprint of the rushes was organised from the original negatives and these were duly delivered to me the next morning in the cutting room. I worked my way through them, knowing it was a last resort, but hell-bent on averting disaster. After some twelve hours of non-stop concentration, willpower somehow triumphed over the seemingly impossible and every shot was matched back to the soundtrack, effectively creating a replacement cutting-copy. I drove immediately to the neg-cutters and handed it over personally since I wasn't prepared to risk it going missing again. The next morning I invited Jack to view the first print delivered by the laboratory and we sat and watched it with shared feelings of relief.

I will never know if that first cutting-copy was ever found, but on the positive side it if it had never gone missing I would not have had the opportunity to display my conjuring skills in creating a second version from memory that ensured transmission on its scheduled day, at its scheduled time. A career salvaged at the eleventh hour, and a memo from Jack to Ken Cooper thanking me for my 'dedicated work and commitment without which the programme would never have been ready in time,' which might have been loosely translated as 'Harvey messed up but somehow managed to save the day by the skin of his teeth.' Despite the memo, I could still sense a large question mark hovering over my head, since a great many executives must have been bricking it over the very real possibility of missing an important transmission slot and heads would most certainly have started rolling along the corridors of Television Centre.

I was unsure if any more projects would be forthcoming after that debacle, but a month or so later Ken offered me a *Horizon* special, possibly as a thank-you for resolving the Luther King crisis, or more likely because this new commission, *A Touch of Sensitivity*, involved editing a mass of hidden camera footage, a genre I was particularly familiar with. Thankfully post-production went like clockwork, culminating in a successful show that attracted a high audience rating and produced my second positive memo, this time from producer Stephen Rose. It was much-needed and timely redemption.

SLIDING DOORS

Many of us arrive at a defining moment when our lives can veer one way or the other and we either have to make a momentous decision or fate steps in and makes it for us; a moment when our future can become instantly defined - or disappear in a heartbeat. It certainly doesn't pay to be complacent as you work your way along your chosen career path. As a freelance I bobbed and weaved through a minefield of company politics and policy changes, unexpected editorial decisions and budget cuts, to the point where I never knew quite what was going to happen next. I repeatedly saw myself walking along a swaying tightrope, trying to keep my balance, but knowing that what goes up might just as easily come down – and take my life in a different direction to the way I hoped it would turn out.

My own unexpected sliding door moment came in 1980. *Horizon* had provided interesting work for me for several months, and although I had managed to keep my reputation intact despite the Luther King debacle, an incident on Robin Brightwell's *The Black and the Gold*, a documentary about life on a North Sea oil rig, nearly torpedoed me in a way I could never have predicted.

I had been hard at work on the project for about two weeks, Robin having left me with several hours of film to rifle through and put into some semblance of order while he went off to organise his next shoot. It was standard practice for me to view rushes in tandem with the director's notes, then make a first assembly based on my own notes so the director could experience an element of surprise. To that end, my working method was to always create an interesting hook to draw the viewer in, based on the premise that your film needs to assert itself from the outset and let the audience know that the story is a worthy investment of their time. If my first assembly did not contain a scene that fulfilled that purpose within the first three or four minutes I would reach into the body of the film, pull out something more interesting and kick-start the programme with it. This often meant slicing some of the action in half and creating a cliff-hanger that would be concluded at a later point. It is not an approach that has the approval of every editor and director but is a practice that stood me in good stead for nearly fifteen years as an editor on network television, and for many years after that as a director.

The first assembly of *The Black and the Gold* was running at some twenty minutes over length, which wasn't unusual for a one-hour documentary, and we had arranged to view it one evening at seven o'clock. The cutting room itself was part of a private house that contained two or three other cutting rooms, hired by editors who were also feverishly trying to hit deadlines. It was, however, a fairly old house and although kept in reasonably good decorative order and maintained on a regular basis, still harboured areas of neglect that you would find in any property of a certain age.

Just before seven, I decided to nip upstairs and spend a penny. The toilet was located on the first floor, and although not particularly large and in need of a coat of paint here and there, served its purpose. I locked the door, noticed that the sash-cord window was shut and moved over to release the catch. What happened next was as unexpected as it was swift, and brought tears to my eyes. The top window suddenly collapsed and crashed down as the sash-cord rope snapped, the downdraught taking my fingers with it and trapping them between the two giant windowpanes. The pain, unsurprisingly, was excruciating. There isn't any room between two window frames to accommodate a set of fingers, yet mine were wedged firmly in, mangled and bloody and with no hope of an early release.

I wriggled about, the pain getting worse by the second, with absolutely no idea how to resolve the situation. As I stood trapped in the little bathroom the thought crossed my mind that the other editors may have left for the night, leaving me alone in the house. Even if they were still on the premises, none of them were responding to my shouts, and the door was locked anyway. It didn't look good.

There was the added problem that Robin would arrive at seven o'clock expecting to view his rough-cut, but with no sign of his editor. I assumed he might hang about for maybe half an hour, perhaps even view the edit without me, and then leave, more than a little pissed off. Even if he came looking for me and by chance came up to the first floor loo and discovered my plight, he would have to find a way to get me out and that would not be the best of starts with a new producer. Then I realised it could be far worse, because what if the other editors had left and Robin didn't actually turn up? Or what if he turned up but couldn't get in because the front door was locked? Not to mention the mounting discomfort that was numbing my senses. At best, I could possibly stand the pain for an hour or so but it was inconceivable I could last through the night.

And then a miracle happened. After ten minutes of mental and physical anguish, a light snapped on in the little kitchenette opposite the courtyard and a face appeared at the window. It was Chris, one of the editors, who had gone in to deposit some coffee cups in the sink before leaving for home. As soon as he saw me his face creased into horror, as if he was experiencing my pain for himself. He stood transfixed for a few moments, his mouth trying to form words that wouldn't come, then raced around the corridor to join me, albeit on the other side of the toilet door. Several seconds of pushing, kicking and shoving made no impact whatsoever and he quickly reassessed the situation. His immediate thought was to call the fire brigade, but that would be as good as turning a spotlight on me and giving full media coverage in the BBC staff magazine, along with a few column inches in the local newspaper. Alarm bells might start ringing along the corridors at Lime Grove about my predilection for generating unnecessary complications on a production, which wouldn't be wise, so I suggested it might be worth trying to find a way up to the window himself rather than bother the emergency services.

He disappeared for what seemed like an eternity before emerging in the courtyard below with a ladder, held at one end by a neighbour who I had seen on a couple of occasions mending his bike in the basement garden. They wasted no time in hoisting it up to the window and Chris clambered up it, armed with two hefty screwdrivers I had advised him he might need to prise my fingers out. He pushed the screwdrivers between the two frames and twisted them. Eventually I was able to slide my fingers from the wreckage and stepped back into the bathroom feeling pleased that they were still in one piece.

I sat down on the loo to recover for a few minutes, and then unlocked the door as Chris arrived back at the top of the stairs. He looked at my mangled fingers in disbelief and suggested I go to the hospital immediately. But I had far more pressing things on my mind, like had Robin arrived?

'Yes, he has, he came in when I went to get the ladder.'

'You didn't…?'

'No, he doesn't know. I didn't have time to stop anyway.'

That was the marvellous thing about film editors. They had an amazing capacity for closing ranks where producers and directors were concerned.

And so it was that I slipped back into the cutting room as though nothing had happened and we watched the film together. As Robin took notes I nursed my swollen fingers and damaged pride and gave silent thanks that disaster had been averted.

There is no question that if Chris had not been around that night and I had been forced to endure twelve or more hours of agony, my hands may have been permanently damaged, along with my chances of having a future in the broadcasting industry. As a professional it's always important to retain an air of dignity at all times, appear to be in control no matter what chaos might be going on around you, and not reveal to anyone that you should never be let within a mile of heavy machinery or sash-cord windows. It's also important to remember that it would be unwise to take anything for granted in a world where anything can happen and your life can instantly be turned upside down.

It's also true that, out of the blue, everything can be put back on track, with opportunities opening up that you equally could not have foreseen.

I had spent some eighteen months editing on the *Horizon* series and although everything was going well, the fickle world of television eventually exercised its customary mugging. Extensive budget cuts meant that many productions were being moved back in-house to be edited by members of staff, which meant my current contract would be my last for some time. I took on a short-term project with Video Arts, the company John Cleese founded in 1972, to edit some of their corporate comedy presentations featuring Cleese and John Bird, then took a three month assignment at the BBC staff training unit where I helped aspiring directors edit their first films. One of them, Eric Abrahams, recommended me to a Dutch producer, Ludi Boeken, who had just set up his own company, Belbo Films, in London and was looking for an editor. Ludi was an experienced investigative journalist with an impressive track record. He had started out as a war correspondent for BBC and Dutch TV in the Middle East followed by assignments in South and Central America and Africa. He subsequently directed over 25 investigative documentaries, including the Emmy Award winning *Who Killed Georgi Markov* (BBC Panorama), the prize-winning *The Other Face of Terror* (Channel Four) and *Gypsyland* (Channel Four), all covering Human Rights subjects as well as terrorism, arms trade and torture. He was one of the few to be granted an interview with Augusto Pinochet during the Chilean dictator's reign of terror and Ludi's reputation had attracted investment for numerous documentaries.

My first series with Belbo Films, *The Multinationals*, examined the contentious practices of large corporations throughout Europe, in particular the dumping of outdated medicines on the third world, and set the ball rolling for a year long association with Ludi on a number of excellent projects, including the 1980 documentary *I Captured Eichmann*, which we made with the assistance of Peter Malkin, a member of the Israeli Secret Service operating under the alias of Eli Man. Malkin had helped to catch the notorious war criminal Adolf Eichmann in Argentina in May 1960 and taken him to Jerusalem for trial. He took great pride in being a master of disguise, carrying false wigs and moustaches with him wherever he went. He was one of many informed and high-profile activists that Ludi recruited to add credibility to his films and it was an honour to work with all of them. During our time together Ludi talked enthusiastically about various projects he was keen to get off the ground in the UK and I was excited by his plans for Belbo, which would have guaranteed a continuing association for the foreseeable future.

Unfortunately, he and his English girlfriend split up and several months later he married the renowned French journalist Annette Levy-Willard, shut up shop and moved his entire operation to Paris. I hadn't seen *that* coming.

I had enjoyed every minute of working with Ludi and valued his friendship, so understandably I was devastated when our association came to an end. Ludi is one of many dedicated journalists I have been privileged to work with over the years and whilst it would be inappropriate for me to single out any one of them, Ludi's integrity and perseverance in the most demanding of situations served as a life lesson to me in the importance of holding people to account. His wedding in Paris was the last time I saw him, closing a fulfilling and rewarding chapter on my editing career. 1980 also marked the end of my wonderful run of BBC contracts and I didn't work for the Corporation again for more than twenty years.

My biggest adventure, though, was waiting just around the corner.

REALITY CHECK

The eighties ushered in an era that brought us *Dallas*, Ronald Reagan, Margaret Thatcher, Kickers, the Filofax, the Commodore 64 and The Rubik Cube. Videotape was gradually taking over from film as a primary communications tool, even though it was still very much in its infancy, having not yet achieved digital status. Laptop computers and mobile phones were looming on a distant horizon but yet to make any meaningful impact on our lives. The technological revolution, however, was well under way.

Two TV professionals who had worked at the forefront of hi-tech innovation were Michael Blakstad, producer of *Tomorrow's World*, and the show's presenter, Michael Rodd. They had decided to leave the BBC in 1981 to set up their own company, Blackrod, specialising in science-based television shows and corporate video production, having secured initial seed money from a Japanese company to make an international series about herbs and spices. *The Spice of Life* was to be broadcast on the newly formed Channel Four, headed by Jeremy Isaacs, my former boss, with filming taking place throughout the world, on a budget that today's independent filmmakers can only dream about.

The first I heard about the new company, operating from Clipstone Street in London with its own edit suite and technical areas, conference room and offices, was when Blakstad's production manager, Roger Wilson, contacted me to say that Dave Zeigler at the BBC had recommended me for the role of Supervising Editor on the spices series and would I be interested. By now I was used to people asking rhetorical questions like 'would this project be of interest?' but I'd learned to play it casually and not appear too eager in case it weakened my bargaining position. An initial meeting with the two Michaels went well, the price and contract agreed once I was assured that *The Spice of Life* was to be shot and edited on film and not the new-fangled video format, of which I had very little experience and no particular desire to acquire any.

Colin Barratt, an editor I had met a few years earlier at Thames TV, joined me on the project and we assembled and edited our way through thirteen half hour programmes, viewing countless hours of rushes, including a Maharajah's banquet in India, saffron harvesting in La Mancha, Spain, and the annual chilli cook-off in Terlingua, Texas, all within six months. Our Japanese clients came over to the UK for meetings at regular intervals during this time, bringing gifts in the form of computer games the size of a credit card (a particular novelty at the time) and taking us to supper at the most exclusive Japanese restaurants. Whilst it was hugely enjoyable, the initial rough-cut viewings did not go so smoothly. As objective filmmakers we were committed to making programmes that were informative and entertaining, and not designed to endorse particular brands of herbs and spices. This became a bone of contention for much of the production run; bearing in mind that product placement had not yet become acceptable to the broadcasting authorities at that time.

Another potential setback that surfaced a few months prior to transmission was that a new consortium, Television South, won the ITV franchise to broadcast in the south of England – which Michael Blakstad was a part of. Several weeks of organised chaos ensued as Michael took up his new post as Director of Programmes in Southampton and Blackrod became an autonomous subsidiary of Television South. A new Chief Executive, Clive Moffatt, a former Treasury economist and financial editor at the BBC, was wheeled in to run the company and to complete the funding still needed for *The Spice of Life*, alongside Jill Roach as Head of Production.

None of us saw *that* coming.

We now had the problem of appeasing the Japanese whilst dealing with a union that suspected Blackrod, as an autonomous subsidiary, might become a back-door for making cut-price independent programmes for the ITV network outside of their control. The Channel 4 deal for *The Spice of Life* had been set up long before the Television South franchise was awarded and although Blackrod had no problems making programmes for the BBC and Channel 4, the door was firmly closed to ITV by the union, which meant a stack of interesting project proposals were suddenly dead in the water. I had no particular gripe with the ACTT wanting to protect their technicians at a regional broadcaster from losing out on commissions because of the fear that Blackrod might offer programmes to the network at lower prices, but it was a one-way scenario, with no possibility of anybody who was employed at Blackrod being offered the opportunity to work on commissioned TV programmes at Television South. I also have no issue with a fair day's pay for a fair day's work, whatever a person's religion, race or gender - I sat on the ACTT Freelance Shop Committee for a while in an effort to promote and foster healthy working relationships throughout the industry - but there were times when I felt the union was being unnecessarily belligerent in an attempt to flex its muscles. The fact that a group of staff technicians in privileged, well-paid, secure, employment could block their fellow technicians from having a share of the production pot whilst dictating the modus operandi of their employers told me that the writing was on the wall. When battle lines are drawn and opposing sides cannot find a fair and reasonable solution to their differences, they are invariably on a collision course that it is unlikely to end well.

Undeterred, Michael Rodd kept his allegiance to the company and Jill and Clive forged ahead establishing links with a diverse range of blue-chip corporations. These ranged from banks and building societies to high street retailers and airlines, and within a few months they had accrued an impressive portfolio, making Blackrod one of the top media communications companies in the UK.

I had kept my head down whilst Blackrod weathered the storm, working to a tight transmission deadline for the Spices series, knowing that the company's TV production arm needed to present a quality production to prove its broadcast potential. Our Japanese investors had made several trips to check on progress but I knew they were keen to meet with our new Head of Production to make sure that everything was still on track. One day I was summoned to the meeting room, where Jill, Clive and Sheldon Greenberg, one of our producers, newly arrived from Canada, were sat at a large round table alongside six of the Japanese contingent, all of whom beamed at me expectantly as I entered. Jill pointed to an empty chair and I sat to await instructions. 'Please explain to Mr Shaboaka,' she said tersely, 'that we cannot make television programmes by substituting inspiring scripts for a shopping list of products that they would like us to endorse.'

I hastily surmised the situation. There had obviously been an hour or two of discord as the Japanese contingent had presented Jill with a list of requirements for each of the Spices shows in an attempt to assume editorial control of the series and promote their products. Jill was having none of it and wanted me to clarify just why this was not possible. I decided to take the diplomatic approach, suggesting that we had a responsibility to our audience to offer an interesting and stimulating series of programmes, unhindered by objectives that might diminish the energy and dynamics of the stories. Mr Shaboaka and his companions smiled and nodded but countered by saying that since they were making a substantial financial investment in the programmes it was only fair that their herbs and spices should take centre stage. Jill was insistent that the stories should take centre stage, with the spices forming a natural complement to the cooking scenes and the historical perspective, a debate that carried on for another half an hour before Sheldon threw out a lifeline by suggesting that he and I edit together a trailer from the rushes that had been filmed and logged so far and screen it before our visitors returned to Japan. They agreed, which was just as well, because if they had pulled out at this stage it would have been nothing short of disaster.

For two days we rifled through the rushes logs, picking out interesting scenarios, and Sheldon wrote a short promotional script that would illustrate how both stories and product could work in harmony without the need for any overt product selling.

When the five-minute teaser was finally edited, Edward Woodward, the actor, recorded a voice track, some appropriate music was laid in, and we arranged a screening for our visitors on the morning of their departure. They were immediately transfixed by the unfolding imagery; a fusion of exquisite photography that embraced tradition, history and food, bound together by a voice track that gave structure and authority to a fascinating global story that left nobody in any doubt as to the role herbs and spices played in our cultural heritage and their importance today. Mr Shaboaka thanked us, said he was very much looking forward to seeing the final edits, and set off for the airport with his colleagues, secure in the knowledge that we could be left to complete the films to a standard that would make everybody happy. Which confirmed the wisdom of the Japanese proverb: *a lantern cannot light until someone strikes a match.* Sheldon Greenberg, thankfully, always carried an ample supply of matches with him.

Considering the vast organisational complications involved in sending film crews all over the world, there were very few production crises on *The Spice of Life*. The only unforeseen situations involved an Argentinean director who suddenly had his assets frozen when England declared war on Argentina in April 1982, leaving him stranded without the means to pay for even a cup of tea until the company could bail him out - and a cameraman who fell from a tree whilst filming a nutmeg-picking sequence in the Moluccas, which resulted in a broken arm and a two-week delay while the camera was being fixed.

Nothing too serious all things considered, and with such beautifully filmed and extraordinary footage, Edward Woodward reading the voice-over and Carl Davis scoring the music, it was unlikely to fail. The only spanner in the works was the re-scheduling of the first episode to go on air in Channel Four's first week of transmission – two weeks earlier than planned – resulting in the cancellation of a magazine colour spread *The Observer* had been planning that would have helped enormously to launch the series.

Once all thirteen transmission copies had been delivered and began to broadcast it was time for me to take stock once more. The majority of the company's output was now on videotape but video editing held no appeal for me, since it was a relatively slow and cumbersome medium at that time. Fortunately, because I had steered *The Spice of Life* through to a successful conclusion in spite of heavy content demands made by our Japanese clients, along with a certain degree of creative disparity between the five programme directors, Clive and Jill were keen for me to stay with the company. They knew I had ambitions to move on to directing so Jill took a chance and offered me my first directing project: a documentary commissioned by the Salmon Growers' Association.

The film had been proposed as a day in the life of ordinary people who fished and cooked salmon in a variety of ways, with scenes featuring a gillie supervising an angler on the Isle of Skye, a banquet at the Skeabost Hotel, a salmon buffet at Henley Royal Regatta, kedgeree being made by parents at a school sports day, salmon preparation at a cookery school in West London, and the fish being smoked at Goldstein's smokery in the East End of London. These scenes would be intercut with general activity at salmon farms up and down the Highlands of Scotland, where the breeds were being farmed to ensure plentiful supplies for the future. It was a tremendous opportunity for me to kick-start my directing career.

Research and recces were completed without incident in less than three weeks, with location visits to the schools and the smokery and an extensive road trip through the Highlands to decide which fish farms would be best suited for our filming purposes. Organising the filming schedule also proved to be an effortless task and so, in June 1983, with the crews booked and Colin Barratt assigned to the editing, I set off with my production assistant, Suzy, on a flight to Inverness on a bright and clear blue-sky Sunday, confident that the project would be nothing less than a resounding success. Such is the wishful thinking of the inexperienced director who has never been let loose on the wider world to face the unpredictable nature of documentary filmmaking and all that it can throw at him.

At Inverness Airport we picked up a hire car, dismayed that the weather had now turned from bright sunshine to a low swirling mist but headed, undaunted, for the ferry at Mallaig, praying that the fog would clear by the time we reached the Skeabost Hotel. It was three hours of driving hell as the fog became denser with each passing mile so by the time we pulled into the car park at Skeabost Bridge we had endured a painfully slow journey and could hardly see a foot in front of us. My first concern was that it would be impossible to film in such conditions, especially as the next morning I was scheduled to take a six-hour helicopter flight over the Highlands, filming fish farms from the air. I cursed the fact that Skye was our first port of call and that there was no immediate Plan B. It was my first harsh lesson in scheduling, which is always to factor in weather cover whenever possible, allowing for a switch between exteriors and interiors, or even locations. We had planned to film the interior salmon banquet in the afternoon at the hotel on Tuesday, preceded by a fishing sequence by the River Snizort, but we had no idea how long the fog would linger. Even if it was possible to switch the two days, we still needed our

Scottish cameraman, Mike Herd, at the Skeabost before we could begin filming – and he was booked to come over with his sound recordist in the helicopter, which was currently grounded at Inverness.

I was in quiet despair, watching my first directing assignment unravel faster than I could have believed possible. I sat down with Suzy to examine the alternatives but we were thwarted whichever way we worked the permutations. Assuming Mike Herd could find a way to get to Skeabost Bridge by morning and we could pull the banquet and fishing scenes forward by a day and swap them on the filming timeline, there was still the added problem that sixty or so guests for the banquet were booked into the Skeabost for Tuesday afternoon and would not be available Monday morning. I retired to bed, exhausted by our efforts to rework the jigsaw puzzle, knowing the entire project was in deep trouble and possibly unsalvageable.

At breakfast the next morning we sat in the dining room, staring at a wall of white where the beautiful Loch Snizort should have been. The filming schedule lay on the table, unchanged from the previous night and likely to stay that way. The only thing that had become clearer were the ramifications, and cost, of abandoning the Scottish trip and moving it to the end of the schedule – our remaining option if we were to meet appointments at the cookery school, the sports day, and Henley Royal Regatta, which only had a three-day filming window at best.

And then a miracle happened. The helicopter pilot, who had been giving me regular updates since

7am, telephoned to tell me he had received a more favourable weather report and was flying out with the cameraman and sound recordist to pick me up. I could hardly contain my elation at this unexpected turn of events; so ecstatic that I didn't even consider the dangers of flying at speed, over mountains and valleys in intermittent fog, at the mercy of three and a half tons of vibrating steel, with a pilot who had clearly lost his marbles. But never mind about instant death, the schedule was back on track.

So I took the flight without a second thought, completely focused on enjoying the experience and excited about capturing those first few vital sequences that were essential to the telling of the story. It was an excitement that was to be short-lived. After an hour of skimming in and out of fog, skirting around endless snow-covered mountains, I began to feel nauseous and quite scared. When there are no people on a mountainside, there is no sense of scale, particularly from the air. We could have been three miles or three feet away from a jagged rock face, I had no way of knowing, but the pins and needles in my feet told me I might have trouble completing my aerial inauguration.

On five or six occasions the pilot had to land in the middle of nowhere so I could disembark and walk around in an effort to pull myself together. I have erased much of that day from my mind, but I do recall sitting on a Scottish hillside, in the freezing cold, being observed by a pilot, a cameraman and a sound recordist who must have wondered what on earth had possessed the production company to land them with such a rookie director. For my part it was a rude awakening. How easy it had been to watch men like Mick Burke scale crevasses and ice caverns from the comfort of a centrally-heated cutting room, or journalists like Ludi Boeken putting themselves at risk interviewing despots like Augusta Pinochet, or documentary filmmakers rowing in canoes down crocodile-infested rivers in search of lost tribes – all images on celluloid that did not capture the smell of fear and the dangers that were a very real threat to their personal safety. And here I was, coming to terms with the fact that if I was going to be a successful director, such fears would have to be overcome and all challenges faced head on, because very little of it was ever going to be easy.

It would be an understatement to say that I worked through the day full of apprehension but as I was to discover, events have a curious way of balancing themselves out. When we arrived back late afternoon at the hotel, the sun had come out to welcome us, the mist had dispersed, and Suzy reported that everyone had confirmed they would be available for filming the next day. The worst was over; I had been rewarded for flying into the jaws of death, committed to the cause and doing my bit for salmon lovers everywhere. And when we viewed the rushes back in London a week later, the aerial views of the salmon farms looked amazing; the mist miraculously parting at each farm to reveal the kind of beautifully lit, lyrical shots you could never achieve in any other light.

So, every cloud often *does* have a silver lining – even the ones you find yourself hurtling through at a hundred and thirty miles an hour, propelled by rotor blades, aeronautical know-how and a good dollop of luck. More importantly, making the transformation from editor to director had fulfilled a lifetime ambition and most of the creative journey that followed was to be another diverse mix of adventure and fulfilment, interviewing people I admired but never thought I would actually meet, at locations to which the general public would never normally be allowed access.

There would be times when the pressure would get to me, particularly abroad during long days that hijacked my sense of humour with communications difficulties, geographical problems and an overload of bureaucracy. Before foreign trips appeared on the agenda, however, there was a long list of corporate presentations that had been building up in my absence, which meant I could now work alongside many of the experienced producers on the payroll at Blackrod with growing confidence.

COLOUR MY WORLD

The making of the Dulux promotional film *At Home with Colour* at an Edwardian house in Richmond, Surrey, in June 1983, came as a timely reminder that you can never take anything for granted in the capricious world of television.

Julie Peasgood, an actress who was later to make her mark on TV series such as *Brookside, Holby City* and *The Bill,* played a homeowner who visualised the various colour schemes she might like to have in her new home. The colours were to be added later in post-production so that they could be 'magicked' on screen as the various colour combinations presented themselves. The simple solution would have been to paint the entire house chromakey green so that Julie could physically walk in front of the walls, enabling us to put all the backgrounds in afterwards at the edit. Unfortunately, computer keying using the kind of non-broadcast equipment that was available to us at the time was not as sophisticated as it is today, so unless we could guarantee the green screen was lit completely evenly, with no shadows, on walls inside a real house and not a controlled studio environment, there was a risk of 'fringeing' around Julie's body. The answer was to take shots of the walls *without* Julie standing in front of them so we could wipe in various colour combinations later at the edit, then physically paint her 'chosen' colour onto the walls for the shots where she could be seen hanging up pictures and mirrors. This meant we had to fit the entire filming schedule around a small team of professional decorators who worked ahead of us, painting the appropriate colours onto the walls. Since this took much longer than anticipated we invariably arrived at each room and had to spend valuable time literally watching paint dry before we could do any filming. We also had to contend with the Dulux Dog (an incarnation of the original, to be voiced post-filming by actor Michael Elphick) stopping in the middle of takes to turn its nose up in disgust at the smell and one incident when it stepped into a tray of Midnight Blue, leaving a trail of unique but unwanted paw prints over the hall carpet that had to be hastily cleaned up with a bucket and sponge.

Julie managed to keep morale going with a string of humorous stories, but the owners of the house were beginning to suffer a distinct sense-of-humour-failure, even though they were having their entire house repainted for free. A point worth mentioning here: think carefully before hiring out your house to a film crew. It may sound exciting and life enriching, a jolly jape and financially rewarding, but that's bullshit. It'll turn your life upside down, have you tearing your hair out, have sections of your dwelling looking like a hurricane has just passed through and leave you bemoaning the fact that you ever let a film crew anywhere near the front door. In extreme cases you could be emotionally scarred for life.

By about six in the evening we had set up in the living room for the main filming block. Story-wise it was supposed to be midday, and although we were fortunate to have ample light streaming in through the windows, we knew it wouldn't last. Apart from fighting the clock we were also beginning to suffer the effects of paint and white spirit fumes, which caused me to plunge my arm into a litre of white undercoat before treading on a lid coated with a generous helping of Harvest Gold. I had paint all over my clothes and had to wrap myself in a dustsheet to avoid contaminating the furniture and fittings and inflicting any further damage on myself or my surroundings. By nine o'clock the Dulux Dog had given up on us and retired to his basket, with the owners of the house following suit at about midnight. By one in the morning we were still hard at it, with Nic Morris, the cameraman, having to rig up a large light outside in the front garden to simulate the bright sunshine that had been with us when we began filming. This attracted a group of drunks who had been wandering the streets in search of trouble and now congregated by the front window hurling abuse and empty beer cans at us.

As a consequence, half the neighbourhood was woken up, the dog started barking, the police were called and the drunken gang eventually dispersed. Completing the filming in the face of periodic aggravation, paint fumes and general fatigue took a mighty effort on everyone's part but as is the case with most of my near-disaster experiences, the final show gave no indication of our ordeal during those eighteen hours of filming. Thanks to the combined professionalism of the actors and the crew, *At Home with Colour* turned out to be a successful promotion for the new Dulux colour range. The only sting in the tail occurred when the owners came downstairs the following morning, decided they didn't like the new colour scheme, and asked the decorators to put the entire house back the way it was.

At least I was spared the indignity of having to sit and watch them do it.

HEAVY METAL FATIGUE

Although broadcast productions were not on the agenda at Blackrod for a while we did shamelessly borrow a few popular television programme formats for our corporate production slate. *In at the Deep End*, for example, a TV show that had been running for a couple of years featuring famous people thrown into unusual situations, was adapted for our purposes as *In at the Deep End at Marks and Spencer*, with presenter Sarah Kennedy taking up temporary employment at one of the famous retailer's London stores, looking behind the scenes and observing customer liaison. Because we needed to hide the camera on a trolley so the customers were not aware we were filming, the cameraman suggested that he could set the camera to record and leave me to wheel it around and follow Sarah, since I had a clearer idea of what I was looking for content-wise. I agreed but after following Sarah through the store for a good ten minutes and with no on-screen participation on her part, I stopped and asked her why she was not approaching customers and engaging them in conversation. 'I haven't seen the cameraman for a while so I assumed you'd stopped filming,' she said by way of explanation. 'Ah,' was all I could say as I realised with more than a degree of embarrassment that I hadn't kept her in the loop and explained that I was doing the filming in his absence – another lesson learned. On future projects I always made sure that everyone involved in the production was aware of what was going on every step of the way. Whilst it turned out to be another rewarding shoot, presentations like this made no particular creative demands on me, and after a while I was keen to take on something more challenging.

It came out of nowhere one Monday morning when Michael Rodd walked into the office and asked me if I would be interested in covering a four-camera shoot at Hammersmith Odeon. It transpired he had spent the weekend in Newcastle with an old colleague at Neat Records, Dave Wood, whose company managed the black metal group, Venom, and wanted their latest concert filmed for distribution on video. Michael must have decided that my brief excursions into multi-camera land on a couple of our road shows made me the man for the job, even though my experience was somewhat limited. It sounded like an interesting proposition and a brief diversion from our traditional assignments into untried territory, so I jumped at the chance.

The recording of Venom's *7th Date of Hell* tour at Hammersmith Odeon in June 1984, and the subsequent events it spawned, will forever stay etched in my memory. It took three hours ahead of the concert to rig the four monitors and vision mixing desk at the back of the upper circle, with cables running to the three cameras set up around the circle and stalls, and the one on the stage itself. Venom were not on hand for rehearsals. Apparently they were recovering from sunburn following a recent trip to Los Angeles. Being of Dark Satanic persuasion they only usually emerged at night to play at gigs dressed in their customary black leather, complete with studs and swinging metal chains, so spending a day basking half-naked in the sizzling Californian sunshine was always going to end badly.

In their absence we had to second guess what might happen during the performance - not an ideal situation considering that lighting changes, moving platforms and pyrotechnics were involved. At the witching hour, in front of a live audience, the support group went through their set, which gave us a chance to set sound and lighting levels and rehearse camera shots. Amazingly, the cameramen could hear me through their earpieces despite the noise, and all equipment feeds were given the thumbs up by the technical crew.

Then Venom appeared on stage and the disadvantages of not rehearsing with them became all too apparent. The audience erupted in hysteria, the sound levels shot up three million decibels, and the gates of hell opened up. In a panic I shouted into my microphone to make sure the cameramen could still hear me and was relieved to see the cameras nod up and down in response. Whilst I couldn't actually hear the crew reply via their own microphones it was vital that I could shout instructions to them, and they responded magnificently.

For an hour and a half the noise continued unabated as we recorded the audio onslaught of such evergreen crowd-pleasers as *Buried Alive, Bloodlust, Nightmare* and *Welcome to Hell,* while the building shook, and the crowd went manic. Having your brain hammered for an eternity can have the curious advantage of sucking you into the madness of the moment and we completed our mission at about ten o'clock, feeling unexpectedly pleased with the coverage.

With high adrenaline levels still pulsing through my body I briefly attended an after-show function in the dressing room, but feeling somewhat intimidated by the band's menacing stage persona, made an early departure in the hope that I could erase the thumping sounds still going on in my ears. Half an hour later I arrived home, climbed wearily into bed, and lay listening to the pounding sounds of hell bouncing off the walls of my mind.

I discovered next morning that Venom had accidentally burned the Hammersmith Odeon ceiling during one of the pyrotechnic displays and were banned from playing there for a year. I then had to return to Newcastle with the master videotapes so that the sound technicians could overdub some of the live recording using the original studio tracks in order to reduce the amount of audience noise. And that, I thought, would be the end of my heavy metal experience and all its associated mania.

Except that a month later an excited Dave Wood contacted Michael to say that Polygram were pleased with the outcome of the Hammersmith Odeon video and wanted to commission a one-hour special featuring four bands who were under contract to them, including Venom, showing stage performances intercut with fantasy pop promo-type location scenarios. When Michael suggested it might be good fun for me to head up to Newcastle and spend a week on the road with some heavy metal fanatics I should have stopped and thought long and hard about the ramifications. But I didn't and *Metal City* went into pre-production just a few days later. I drove up to Newcastle and met with Dave Wood, who outlined the brief. 'Twelve tracks, four bands, three songs each.' And that was it. Unquestionably the shortest brief I've ever had from a client, and although it turned out Venom had some firm ideas on how their songs should be storyboarded, I was given free rein to create any fantasy sequences I liked for the other three bands. Apart from anything else, there wasn't time to involve eleven band members in group discussions about filmic ideas, so I spent the following three days studying the song lists for Saracen, Warfare and Avenger, exploring a local area that was unfamiliar to me, and working out visual themes around their song titles, which included *Under the Hammer, We Have Arrived* and *Revenge Attack*.

I was keen to find unusual locations for the playback sequences, so I recced derelict buildings, old theatres and breaker's yards; anything that looked neglected but atmospheric. *Under the Hammer* seemed straightforward enough. I would film the band arriving at a breaker's yard in a clapped-out car, smoke billowing from the interior, watch them tumble out and start playing any metal objects they could lay their hands on, including gear boxes for guitars and old oil cans for drums. My initial thought was to give one of them an iron bar to smash up some cars with, but I later changed that to a sledgehammer. Big mistake.

By the middle of the week I had roughed out some possibilities and Venom turned up at the offices to go over their storyboard for the *Nightmare* track. This involved finding a dwarf and two actors to play the roles of a girl having a nightmare about her fantasy soldier lover who turns into a witch halfway through the song. In the bizarre world of pop promos – especially heavy metal promos – the last thing you apply is any narrative logic. That would make things far too ordered, and this sequence needed to be scary and unsettling.

Fortunately, the lads had some constructive suggestions and were very amenable to storyboard changes and I wasn't half as unnerved by meeting the band as I had been backstage a month earlier at Hammersmith Odeon. Without the heavy make-up, black leather and silver chains, they were just three ordinary northern lads who liked to get up on a stage and perform and I really warmed to them. It was the marketing and the hype that intensified the illusion of Satanic evil; three larger-than-life symbols of hate and vengeance, Cronos, Mantas and Abaddon – real names Conrad, Jeff and Tony - silhouetted against the burning fires of hell on just about every poster and record sleeve you came across. I attempted to organise sensible meetings with the other three bands, but they didn't roll out of bed until well after lunch, after which they put forward zany – and expensive – ideas that had to be simplified if the budget had any chance of staying on track. It was a tricky two weeks, during which I had a nagging doubt in the back of my mind that collectively they would be quite a handful and terrifyingly unpredictable.

Back in London, Michael and I went over my game plan with PolyGram. They were happy with the scenarios but felt some were a bit lame for the target audience. 'We need more sex and violence,' they said as the meeting concluded. 'Life in the raw, aggressive and mean, Newcastle style.' As they said their goodbyes and headed off down the street, Michael and I looked at each other in bemusement. More sex and violence. We had never had a brief like that from a client before and not likely to again.

A week later I was back in Newcastle with Mary, my PA, full of anticipation and trepidation because although I had revised the schedule and rewritten many of the scenes, there was no time for a second recce so it was going to have to be done on the hoof. I met up with the cameraman, Andy Parkinson, equipment supervisor Derek Oliver, and sound recordist Nick Ware at the Post House Hotel, not sure how I was going to outline our seven days on the road with a well-meaning but totally out-of-control bunch of rock musicians. Although Andy was slightly fazed that not all the locations had been identified, nor casting completed, he seemed quite excited about being roped into the selection process rather than be presented with everything set in stone. I avoided elaborating on the violence aspect since I didn't want to freak them out too early, and since I was uncomfortable at the prospect of going on my own to a Newcastle strip club to audition a bevy of naked women, I suggested Mary join me in my quest to select our nubile performers, having explained the scenario. The visuals to Saracen's *We Have Arrived* originally featured the four band members on their way to a gig in their minibus, being stalked by various zombies in vans and cars. I ditched the zombies and replaced them with the girls, who would feature in a series of raunchy, seductive fantasy dance routines. It was a cheaper alternative and unquestionably accommodated the sex requirement.

We completed the selection process at the strip club and met the next morning with Saracen at a quiet spot as far away from human interchange as was possible, on the outskirts of Newcastle. I hadn't had time to alert the police of our intentions so I was keen to get the ball rolling on a road that was well off the beaten track and away from prying eyes. Fortunately, the girls were completely professional about the whole thing – running naked through woods and briar patches and then dancing provocatively for the fantasy scenes later at one of the nightclubs, although I was still relieved when we wrapped at the location. I had spent most of the time worrying that we would be arrested on indecency charges, which would not have been a good way to start day one of a seven day shoot and I certainly wouldn't have relished explaining how it had happened to Clive back at Clipstone Street.

When we retired to the hotel that night, Andy and the boys were still trying to adjust to the off-the-wall, surreal world I'd pitched them into. I hadn't the heart to tell them it was about to get a whole lot weirder.

The first scene of day two featured a girl scantily clad in leather straps and chains smashing a car windscreen with a sledgehammer in the breaker's yard, in theory a straightforward piece of action. My original storyboard for the Avenger song *Under the Hammer* had featured one of the band members demolishing the windscreen, but I factored in the vengeful female to spice up the storyline and, again, promote the sex angle. I stood her at a forty-five degree angle at the front of the car, set Andy in position looking out through the windscreen and shouted 'Action!'

Smash! The sledgehammer was swung at the windscreen with such velocity it instantly shattered, sending shards of glass in all directions and peppering the girl's upper torso so she looked like a bloodied pin-cushion. We spent a good ten minutes picking out the tiny splinters and wiping off the blood, thankful that none had gone anywhere near her face. One of the breaker yard team, who had been standing watching the incident, informed us we had gone about it in completely the wrong way. It's a strange but recurring phenomenon when you are out filming that some wise-arse will point out your shortcomings *after* the event rather than before it. 'She should have stood on the roof and swung it downward in an arc.' He demonstrated, moving his arms in a swift downward movement. 'More effective and much safer.'

I offered to take the girl to the local A & E but she was keen to carry on, as long as she could stand on the car roof as advised. We reset the camera beside a second car and she climbed up on the roof, wielding the sledgehammer menacingly like a war vixen in a post-apocalyptic movie, legs apart, savage intent stamped across her face, and not in the least bit daunted by her previous mishap. She clenched the handle and swung it viciously at the windscreen, smashing it decisively and effectively. I didn't request a second take; what we filmed could not be bettered and I would have been pushing my luck to take the risk. Besides, we now had to focus on the scene with the band arriving in a car that was billowing smoke without asphyxiating any of them.

Co-ordination for this was more difficult than anticipated. The car had no engine so we had to select a location that was on a slope so the vehicle could be pushed into shot against a mangled pile of rusting cars in the background. The band then had to cram themselves inside the car as we pumped smoke into it, with one of them taking responsibility for applying the brakes at the appropriate moment. We filmed four takes of the car rolling into shot and immediately out again as the driver completely mistimed his stop point. On Take Five the car careered out of control as the coughing, spluttering occupants lost all geographical awareness and it swung round, ploughing into our backdrop of twisted metal. This time we needed to tow it back into its start position, which gave the band a chance to recover from the fumes by going off and having a cigarette break. When we were finally ready for another take, the lads decided that careering up and down in a car that was a potential death trap wasn't fun any longer and they made a determined – and successful – effort to hit their mark as the car rolled into shot. Mission accomplished. The rest was relatively easy; the drummer banging away at old oil drums, the lead singer miming to playback using a bent spanner as a microphone and so on.

Everyone took a well-earned lunch break and I went ahead to our next location to make sure I could gain access. The theatre owner had arrived just before me and already opened up, so I walked up the stairs to the balcony and looked out over the stage. The place hadn't been used in years; paper was peeling away from damp, mildewed walls, cobwebs hung in despondent isolation everywhere, rubble was strewn all over the floor. Half the seats had been torn out and it looked abandoned and dilapidated. But it suited my purpose.

Soon after the crew arrived and I could hear them coming up the stairs, fumbling about in the semi-darkness, laughing and giggling. Hysteria had got to them unusually early, though they were going to need their sense of humour if they were to survive the week. I couldn't blame them for thinking it was all excessively weird. Our usual Blackrod expeditions involved interviews, drama training scenarios, or location shoots on industrial estates. Filming in strange, hazardous locations with heavy metal bands was something of a culture shock, so I just hoped they wouldn't consider jumping ship.

Thankfully, the next couple of sequences involved technical challenges that Andy was remarkably adept at: filming stage performance to playback. He had a long track record making pop promos for the likes of Elton John and supervising concerts for musicians such as Jean Michelle Jarre, who used complex lighting rigs, and he was without doubt one of the best hand-held lighting cameramen in the country. His coverage of Saracen playing was visually electric and the stage area looked remarkably atmospheric. No mean feat in such conditions. Considering our near disastrous start, the back-to-back filming of *Under the Hammer* and *Revenge Attack* went better than I could have reasonably expected. Every sequence was captured with inspired camerawork and spirited performances that gave the scenes some real visual energy.

We still had three days to go though and this included a day-long session on the Wednesday in a residential district at a youth theatre that Dave Wood had hired so that we could film the remaining eleven songs to playback. It was a tight agenda, made all the more precarious by a mind-blowing lack of organisation and punctuality on the part of the band members, who wandered in and out at will or went home to wash their hair the very moment I needed them on camera. Not being used to early morning starts and long filming days they invariably turned up looking dazed and disoriented, with little respect for either the budget or the schedule. I had to frequently second-guess them, so it was more by accident than design that we managed to stagger through the day and complete the sequences, though only by filming well into the night. I had been concerned that by two in the morning the neighbours would have had enough of the noise and report us to the authorities. I expected a police raid at any minute but it didn't happen, possibly because the neighbours were afraid there might be consequences upsetting an assortment of very large and angry looking young men who had invaded their street with the sole purpose of creating musical mayhem.

The one incident that might have had serious consequences occurred when Venom's drummer, Tony, organised a pyrotechnic finale to one of Warfare's songs. The spectacular fountains of potassium and sulphur that shot into the air scorched part of the backcloth and partly ignited the bass guitarist's flowing locks, doused by a quick-thinking roadie who emptied the contents of a can of Heineken over him. Thankfully it wasn't anything with higher alcohol content.

The final few days were spent recording scenes for the Venom *Nightmare* track, featuring the dwarf playing a lute and the three actors performing their roles as the soldier, the witch and girl-who-has-nightmares respectively. Still wallowing in his pyrotechnic master-stroke at the youth theatre, Tony arranged various colourful explosions to add visual stimulus to the scene of the girl being chased through the wood by the witch, and my nerves were suitably shredded by the time I finally called a wrap.

We felt surprisingly sad to leave Newcastle. It had been a stressful seven days, with all of us miraculously avoiding arrest, suffering serious injury, being blown to pieces or crushed to death, but we wouldn't have missed it for the world. That said, if Health and Safety regulations were as tight then as they are today I doubt we would have been allowed to film even half of those sequences, if any, in which case *Metal City* would have remained a figment of someone's imagination. I never saw Dave Wood or any of the band members again after that crazy filming period, and whatever those of us with more conventional tastes might think of their music, Venom had a huge global following, a review in The Rough Guide to Rock and Roll declaring that 'If you had to choose just one band as the main driving force behind the black metal scene then Venom would have to figure pretty high on the charge sheet.' Without doubt they were a terrific bunch of lads who given the crew and me the most bizarre yet unforgettable experience of a lifetime.

LARGER THAN LIFE

It was not only performers who defied the conventional and made life more interesting and entertaining with their distinctive take on things. Film and television companies were a hotbed of quirkiness, a magnet for attracting a multitude of highly talented and unique individuals to spice up proceedings. I encountered numerous people whose contribution behind the scenes was often matched by their unexpected and idiosyncratic behaviour. Graham Curtis, for example, was a freelance film editor I bumped into at various regional ITV stations, who had a passion for collecting model railway engines and set up railway tracks along the corridors so that the filmed rushes could be carried from the processing plant at one end of the building to his cutting room at the other; the daily transportation of these rolls of film providing an entertaining diversion for the technical staff and reportedly running to a more reliable timetable than National Rail could ever have managed.

There were others whose contribution to the performing arts was immeasurable, but who were often not given due credit by either the general public or those they worked with. Creatives such as John

Bassett, a director who turned up at Blackrod one day with rushes for a promotional documentary I was due to edit with him for the Performing Right Society. John was an amiable, extremely well-spoken and knowledgeable chap; a veteran of the entertainment circuit whose extraordinary background I was shamefully unaware of. Just as I had not known anything about Hughie Green's chequered past, I was woefully ignorant of the fact that John Bassett had, as a student at Wadham College, Oxford, headed a traditional jazz ensemble called the Bassett Hounds and was subsequently hired by Robert Ponsonby, artistic director for the Edinburgh International Festival and creator of the satirical revue show *Beyond The Fringe.* John had an eye for talent and recommended one of his fellow musicians, Dudley Moore, for the new show, along with writer/performers Jonathan Miller and Alan Bennett. The incomparable Peter Cook completed the line-up, becoming principal writer for the show, which was to play in London's West End and then on Broadway and is widely regarded as seminal to the rise of satire in Britain in the 1960s.

Whilst I, and most of the population, were aware of the Fringe shows and the luminaries who performed in it, I had no idea that John Bassett had not only been the catalyst for such an important part of our comic heritage, but was also involved as an Assistant Producer on the television show *That Was The Week That Was* and had discovered Eric Chappell (author of *Rising Damp, Only when I laugh, Duty Free*, and many other sit-coms) who until that time had been an Internal Audit Clerk for East Midlands Electricity.

John made no mention of his involvement in the legendary Fringe shows when we worked together and I remained blissfully unaware of his influential role in television history until a few months after we had parted company and met up for the occasional lunch. A couple of years later I received a flyer in the post for the hire of a riverboat steam cruiser, which came complete with its captain, John Bassett. John had decided to call time on his creative activities and settle for a less stressful lifestyle, cruising up and down the waterways of France, most particularly the Canal de Bourgogne, in a Dutch hotel barge called *La Belle Aventure*, during which journeys he kept his customers entertained with a collection of amusing stories from his days in TV and theatre. I regret that I never took him up on the offer. I am sure it would have been a fascinating and enlightening experience.

Another colleague whose contribution to the production process was interesting in a more unpredictable way was Roger Chinnery, the man brought in to organise the flow of film into the cutting rooms on *The World at War*. Affectionately known as The Chin, Roger was a charming, well-spoken chap who wore tweed suits and army boots and conducted the logging of rushes and library footage in a military-style campaign of such complexity that few could get to grips with how the system worked other than him. In a master stroke of misguided genius he decided one day, without rhyme or reason, to transfer all of the catalogued film from their tenure inside metal film cans, to cardboard shoe boxes, on the basis that flat boxes would not roll around on the shelves and it was easier to label the sides for faster access. With the logging room now resembling a branch of Freeman, Hardy and Willis, the editors pointed out to Roger that he may have overlooked the fact that the cardboard boxes would become crumpled or torn within a couple of months let alone over a three-year period, and there was an added fire risk. Thankfully he saw the sense in the arguments and returned the film to its safer occupancy inside the film cans and one can only imagine the outcome if Roger's enthusiastic *piece de resistance* had taken place just a few days before Alan Afriat's cutting room caught fire.

And then there was Stuart Hall. Not Stuart Hall the radio and television presenter who underwent a court case in 2014, but Stuart Hall the director and ace practical joker, whose penchant for creative deception and trickery often overshadowed his reputation as a gifted technician.

I had met Stuart at Thames Television in the early seventies when he was film editing on various current affairs shows, including the *Today* programme. None of these programmes had any particular affiliation with the world of light entertainment, with all its glitz, glamour and showbiz razzmatazz, yet despite the fact that Stuart had never directed as much as a single camera location insert, he somehow persuaded his bosses at Thames to offer him a long-term contract as a multi-camera director on comedy revues and high rating shows such as *Opportunity Knocks.*

That was virtually unheard of. Directors on light entertainment shows usually had at least a basic grounding in this specialist genre, whether as floor managers, designers or choreographers, so how Stuart managed to beat the system remains something of a mystery. I remember Peter Dulay expressing his concern at having a director assigned to him who had no experience in the area of light entertainment, but he was won over very quickly, as Stuart displayed a natural aptitude for music and variety and they shared the same mischievous sense of humour.

It was no secret, however, that he was not a devotee of his presenter, Hughie Green, and there were numerous clashes of personality, and creative differences surfaced on a regular basis. Whenever there were problems on the studio floor Hughie would summon over the producer and hold his thumb over his radio mic so that the discussion could not be heard in the gallery. In response, Stuart would request any available sound boom to be maneuvered into a position where the conversation could be picked up without Hughie's knowledge. In the bar one evening Hughie asked Stuart if he could borrow ten pence to phone a friend. Stuart placed two ten pence pieces on the counter and told him to call both of them. It was a jibe that Hughie never forgave him for.

Although Stuart was a highly skilled director, his obsession with practical joking was to bring him into conflict on numerous occasions with his bosses, who didn't approve of his irreverent shenanigans, particularly during recordings of their high-profile ratings winners. Perhaps his most famous and legendary piece of tomfoolery centred on the

117

imaginary Albert Shankshaft. Shankshaft was created by Stuart one morning when he realised that the office situated directly opposite his own had been empty for several weeks and decided it was high time somebody took residence, even if they were only a figment of his fertile imagination. He waited until the head of personnel went away on holiday for a couple of weeks and telephoned one of her juniors, assuming the identity of Albert Shankshaft, a producer who had just been signed on contract, but whose office was bereft of any furniture. Believing an oversight had occurred, the assistant apologised and immediately requisitioned chairs, tables and desks from various parts of the studio lot and had them sent over to the empty office. A telephone was installed that afternoon and for several weeks Stuart adopted a second identity, making calls to various departments requesting stationery, reference books and paintings for the walls. He even had a new carpet fitted. I don't recall how long the joke went on for but I do remember Stuart confessing to me some years later that he began to doubt the wisdom of the joke after he had submitted a form claiming expenses and the payroll department paid them. It was only then that he realised how badly the whole thing could backfire and decided it would be best to go cap in hand to senior management and confess to his misdemeanors before they accused him of fraudulent behaviour.

Stuart probably escaped being fired for his practical joking more times than he cared to remember, and management was becoming increasingly irritated with his fondness for causing disruption and confusion at every opportunity. Jim

Davidson, a comic who had formed a strong working bond with Stuart over the years, once told me that he often sailed too close to the wind and needed to tone down his jokey joy-riding before it had more serious consequences.

Stuart Hall died relatively young, long before he had exhausted his stockpile of the jolly japes that the TV community had been suffering and enjoying for more than a decade. His funeral was attended by some notable figures from the entertainment world, including Davidson, who said some fitting words in tribute, and others who took the opportunity to play the ultimate practical joke on the master prankster, including Matthew Corbett, whose puppet Sooty tapped his magic wand on the side of the coffin, insisting that Stuart should stop mucking about and come out. Ironic that Sooty, a children's television favourite since the 1950s, was 64 years old on 19 July 2012, outliving even the seemingly indestructible Stuart Hall.

There is no doubt that Stuart would have appreciated the joke. He loved television, he loved his job, and he enjoyed indulging in the kind of shock tactics that were meant to take people by surprise but were never intended to offend. The television industry would certainly not be the same without the likes of Stuart Hall and the host of colourful characters who come along to brighten our day when the world sometimes has the habit of collapsing around our ears.

NEW HORIZONS

Life settled back into the more familiar once *Metal City* had been edited and put to bed, although it was far from dull. I was fortunate to be given some interesting projects, which included following a group of people on an action-packed simulated global expedition down rapids, on rollercoasters, and over mountains for Thomson Simulation (an expedition which thankfully I did not have to take for real). Apart from creating simulated adventure rides for the public, Thomson Simulation's main focus was to develop a range of training programmes that allowed pilots to fly sophisticated airplanes and helicopters on hydraulic motion platforms without having to leave the ground. The advancements made in simulation technology today are jaw-dropping, with their range of training software now extended to tanks, trains, trucks, ships and buses, all offering an artificial learning experience in a safe environment without the pressures normally associated with having to learn on the job in the real world. Thomson Simulation was just one of a growing number of corporations that Blackrod helped in promoting their products and their internal communications.

We transformed Midland Bank's Soho branch into a vast jungle, complete with monkeys, plants and cicadas, the scenario featuring an actor hacking his way through the undergrowth until he chances upon a helpful female clerk who offers help and assurance that the Midland can cut through the confusion and offer a clearer sense of direction. It was targeted at staff to familiarise them with the bank's new initiatives so they could help expand their customer base and the idea proved to be a surprisingly effective way of getting the message across. I travelled all over the UK, very often with Michael Rodd, making communications videos for clients aimed specifically at promoting their services or for internal staff training. Within twelve months we had made video presentations for Barclays Bank, Panasonic, General Portfolio, Philips, Sony and Manpower recruitment.

On one unforgettable occasion, during a road show for the Halifax Building Society in Harrogate, the futuristic set exploded, sending smoke wafting across the stage and completely obliterating the set. From behind this curtain of unexpected theatrical smog came Michael Rodd, immaculate in tailored suit, shoes shining, hair perfectly in place, and a calming smile on his face. For several minutes he regaled a hundred captains of industry with tales of mishaps on *Tomorrow's World* that had them rolling in the aisles until the backstage crew had sorted out the problem and were able to continue. Michael was a smooth operator who never got in a flap; the consummate professional, without any doubt. I cannot think of anyone else who could have saved that situation with such control, and in the years that followed I became increasingly impressed with his ability to solve any communication challenge presented to him.

I was also privileged to work with the Beatles' record producer, George Martin, on a presentation to promote his new recording complex in Hampstead, Air Studios, a Grade II listed Victorian church that he was converting. George had previously constructed a studio on Montserrat but Hurricane Hugo had devastated the island and it was forced to close, so all his attention was on promoting Air. When I interviewed George he was totally committed to the new venture and very excited about the possibilities. Off camera we chatted about the Beatles' heyday, he enthusing about the remarkable talent he had been given the opportunity to develop, me recalling my brief encounters with John, Paul and Ringo at the cutting rooms in Old Compton Street. Air Studios is now regarded as one of the foremost recording venues, attracting high profile musicians from all over the world. We filmed the renovation work over six months, culminating in the installation of the mixing desks and consuls in readiness for its official opening with a musical performance of *Under Milk Wood*, in the presence of HRH the Prince of Wales. Nobody would deny George his success. He wasn't just one of the greatest record producers of our times he was a warm-hearted man who gave opportunities to hundreds of recording artists, all of whom have benefited greatly from his advice and mentoring.

It was one of the last projects I directed for Blackrod that was based in the UK. After that, the company's portfolio took on a global reach and before long I was spending more time abroad than at home. And that meant facing a whole new set of challenges - and some hairy escapades.

It began deceptively slowly, with advance sorties, paid for by the clients, to explore potential investment possibilities in regard to promotional material. On most of these trips I was accompanied by producer Sheldon Greenberg, the creative force I had worked with on *The Spice of Life*. Sheldon had previously worked as Senior Writer on *Fast Forward*, an innovative and acclaimed science/technology series for TV Ontario before coming to the UK, and had proved he could turn his hand to almost any creative concept Michael Blakstad or Jill Roach chose to throw at him.

New York was our first port of call, and meetings with the heads of AT&T, the American multinational corporation, who were considering promoting a new telecommunications initiative. I recall very little of our head-banging business sessions, just the experience of being in a city that was so alive you could feel the energy surging beneath your feet. We stayed at a friend of Sheldon's, Jim St Lawrence, in Manhasset, a hamlet in Nassau County on the North Shore of Long Island. When we weren't joining the regular commuter run between Manhasset and New York City for meetings with AT&T, we visited Jim at The New York Institute of Technology where he gave us a demonstration of the kind of advanced digital animated graphics that would later be used on software such as Paintbox, Photoshop and the more sophisticated CGI programs that were to follow. It was worth the trip to New York just to be given such an amazing glimpse into the future.

Although they liked our ideas, AT&T ultimately decided it would be more practical to hire an

American agency to help promote their interests, rather than a UK team who would not be instantly on hand for presentations and briefings. AT&T may have been at the leading edge of telecommunications and Blackrod at the forefront of science-related programming, but in the mid-eighties the internet was not a globally established form of communication, so the use of Skype for conference calls or the emailing of PDF files, videos and graphics was still on the technological wish-list. It was a disappointment, but there were plenty more projects lined up to keep us busy.

We had not been back in the UK long, in fact, before Jill despatched us to Corsica to follow the Rothman's Rally and write a proposal for a documentary about rally driving. *The Rallye de France-Tour de Corse* was first run on the 17th of December, 1956. Of the 43 competitors to start the race, only 24 succeeded in crossing the finishing line, the winners being an all-female crew of Gilberte Thirion and Nadège Ferrier, driving a Renault Dauphine. The rally is held on asphalt roads, and it is known as the "Ten Thousand Turns Rally" because of the dangerous twisty mountain roads, of which we were about to have first-hand knowledge.

It was my first experience of being up close to the razzmatazz that goes with fast cars, their super-rich drivers like the Finnish champion Hannu Mikkola, and the extraordinary entourage that is part and parcel of every event. The daily media circus, the noise, the crowds and the smell of motor oil and burning rubber lingered long after we had left the island. Although we didn't realise it at the time, Corsica in the mid-eighties was one of the most dangerous environments you could find yourself during the rally season. There was virtually no crowd control, and no safety barriers, with some onlookers even standing in the middle of the road as the cars hurtled through at a hundred and fifty miles an hour. Some drivers reported that as they rounded some of the corners they couldn't see the road ahead because it was filled with a seething mass of jostling spectators, most of who ran for cover, whilst others defiantly held out their hands so that they could touch the cars as they sped past.

By 1985, the Group B vehicles favoured by the majority of drivers were the anything-goes cars; built for maximum power and speed and, as such, extremely dangerous. Dynamic new entries that year raised the stakes considerably - at the same time putting hundreds of people at risk. The narrow roads and tight bends, sometimes lined by trees and often bordered by solid rock faces on one side with sheer drops on the other, presented a constant threat to life and limb. Many of the roads provided good grip, but if just one wheel span onto grass or gravel it resulted in a serious loss of traction and there was limited margin for misjudgements, as the smallest of errors could lead to an early and dramatic departure from the race.

The visit, for me, was marked by three distinct events. The first involved being transported between each of the control points in a car driven by an ex rally driver. Because it was essential we arrived at these points ahead of the contestants, our man drove like a bat out of hell on alternative roads, with Sheldon in the back seat not daring to look, and me sitting in the passenger seat with a fixed gaze of terror on my face. On the second day we decided it might be better and less stressful if we hired our own vehicle, which only served to highlight our combined ability to get lost just about everywhere we went. Trying to determine where we should be positioned at any given time so that we could witness crucial stages of the rally turned into a guessing game more than an act of good judgement. We were, however, fortunate to find ourselves at a spectacular incident one night, purely by accident.

We had spent best part of a day driving in low cloud conditions over, round and through the mountains of Corsica, a death-defying experience at the best of times, with sheer cliffs, back-to-back corners, sharp bends and a marked absence of barriers between us and instant death. This was made all the more dangerous by the fact that rally fever had turned everyone into high-speed freaks, and although I have blanked most of those journeys from my mind, I can still hear Sheldon's distressed shouts of 'Jesus that was *close*!' 'Oh *shit!*' and '*Get over!!*' as I gripped the steering wheel in an effort to keep away from the sheer drops that appeared around every corner.

Having arrived at virtually every champion-defining moment a good half an hour after it had happened, we finally trundled into a sleepy village, in the middle of nowhere, in the dark, at about nine o'clock and sat at a garage café to have a coffee and see if we could figure out how to get back to the hotel. In the pitch black. On the same precarious mountain roads.

And then we witnessed something amazing.

Out of the darkness came a rally car driving at high speed, lights blazing, engine roaring, smoke and flames oozing from inside the bonnet. It skidded to a halt in the garage forecourt as its two occupants stumbled out, shouting and cursing. Before we had time to take on board the fact that one of them was Michele Mouton – the most famous female rally driver of all time, accompanied by her co-driver Fabrizia Pons - a team of Audi mechanics sprang out of nowhere, took the car apart and pieced it back together again while we watched open-mouthed. It turned out be a pivotal moment in the rally, with a report of the incident appearing in the newspapers the next day; bereft of any dramatic photographs, naturally, because nobody had been on hand with a camera. Except me that is, a casual onlooker so wrapped up in this once-in-a-lifetime moment that it didn't even occur to him to capture it for posterity and give his camera its place in history.

My Olympus Trip exacted appropriate revenge the next morning.

I was standing on a line of rocks on one of the bends taking action shots as the cars raced towards me. It had seemed a safe enough vantage point but one of the vehicles lost momentary control and when it wobbled slightly I panicked and stepped backwards into thin air. I don't remember much about my fall down the incline, except I ended up lying in a pile of stones and dirt, with my jeans torn at the knee. It took several minutes to find the camera, which had bounced another fifty yards or so beyond my own stop point and although there was no apparent outward damage, it was completely jammed and inoperable. I was helped back up the slope by some concerned onlookers as I cradled a cut arm and hobbled gingerly on a bruised leg, reporting to Sheldon that my one and only roll of film had literally bitten the dust.

Since I was no longer in a fit state to drive, and because Sheldon considered me more dangerous than our rally expert anyway, I was relegated to the passenger seat for the remainder of the trip, taking in the scenery as Sheldon drove at a leisurely pace, well within the speed limits, to the consternation of every other driver on the island, who spent their time honking horns and waving their fists at us. Having witnessed some of the craziest, reckless driving on God's earth for a week, we felt we had earned the right to enjoy the scenery and de-stress and everyone was just going to have to be patient. It was with great relief that we arrived back at the hotel a few hours later without further incident and after being given the all-clear from the unit doctor, I retired to my room to reflect on a truly unforgettable week.

As a postscript, this unregulated mayhem was destined to end abruptly in 1986 after a series of terrible tragedies, which included the loss of Championship star Henri Toivonen, who crashed to his death down a ravine after losing control on a fast early special time stage, and a horrific accident at the Rally Portugal when Joaquim Santos lost control of his Ford RS200 while trying to avoid onlookers on the road, crashing into a human wall of spectators at a hundred and twenty-five miles per hour, killing three and seriously injuring over thirty. Some years later BBC Four made a documentary entitled *Madness on Wheels: Rallying's Craziest Years,* which told how fans, ambition, politics and cars collided with dreadful consequences, and as an on-the-spot-witness I can certainly vouch for its authenticity.

Naively unaware of the full ramifications of what we had witnessed at that time, we returned to London and worked through a proposal to present to Rothmans. It was Sheldon's concept that we finally both agreed on. In simple terms it focused on a couple of local Corsican lads who enter the rally, and I thought it was a stroke of genius. Putting aside all the noise, confusion and chaos that followed us everywhere, we had been impressed watching these no-hopers take to the road in pursuit of their dream, on limited resources and with beaten-up support vehicles being driven on parallel roads and followed by their relatives. Whilst the pro drivers had armies of mechanics waiting en route to administer assistance, the local lads were reliant on their dads and uncles helping them if they got in a fix. Spare tyres, oil and petrol could be delivered eventually, but any serious accidents and they were well and truly side-lined. One distinct advantage was that they knew the roads and would have had plenty of practice time ahead of the main event.

Our proposal didn't exclude the professional drivers; it simply featured the locals in a comparable story that counter-pointed the vast differences in resources and culture, from modest living conditions as opposed to luxury hotels and fine cuisine; from small-scale budgets in contrast to unlimited resources; from girlfriends giving what moral support they could to their boyfriends, to the platoons of attractive female marketing teams promoting rally driving as sexy and seductive. It was, in short, about the triumph of human endeavour in a competition in which winning wasn't as important to the local lads as being part of the spectacle and proving what they were capable of.

But Rothmans didn't go for it. Probably because they didn't think we were being serious. A giant corporation had gone to the trouble and expense of flying two television professionals out to Corsica, presenting them with the cream of world rally driving - and they opt to make a film about two local urchins nobody has ever heard of, racing around the island in a couple of souped-up Fiats. In our defence I think the increasing threats to driver safety on the Corsica circuit may have given them cause to reconsider the notion of making a documentary, but whatever their reasons I still think Sheldon's idea was ahead of its time. *Cool Runnings*, a film based on the Jamaican national bobsleigh team's participation in the 1988 Winter Olympics in Calgary, didn't appear in cinemas until nine years later in 1993, and frankly I think our concept still has legs, or wheels, as either a documentary or a cinema feature. Two lads, awash with passion, up against insurmountable odds, possibly bitter rivals to add drama and extra tension to the story, perhaps one being seduced by an attractive marketing belle to the chagrin of his long-time Corsican girlfriend; maybe even a Mafia sub-plot thrown in for good measure. Intrigue and jealousy, conflict and corruption, all played out against the amazing backdrop of the beautiful Corsican countryside. But I digress, carried away on a wave of indignation, possibly, that our concept was never to see the light of day. A story, perhaps, that one day may still be told.

Following our failure to win two lucrative business contracts, Sheldon and I were channelled into different projects for a while, he serving the needs of clients in the UK, me working on commissioned projects, as opposed to speculative ones, throughout Europe. During that time my Scandinavian Period came and went with a few characteristic mishaps – not all my fault I should add – beginning with a trip to Copenhagen one gloriously hot summer to film a series of promotions, the content of which I cannot now remember but had something to do with container ships and lorries. There had been a delay in the schedule caused by the client being held over in Hamburg and since it was less expensive to keep me in Sweden for three days than fly me back to England and back again, I spent my time sunbathing among picnickers and topless girls in the immensely popular Fælleparken, taking in the museums and art galleries, listening to jazz bands playing by the Slotsholmen Canal and attending open-air concerts in Tivoli Gardens.

After which came two months of travelling across Norway and Sweden making video presentations for travel firms and boat hire companies, until I eventually paid the price for my enforced holiday and gross indulgences in Copenhagen with a horrendous accident in Sweden that could have put paid to my career, and possibly my life, for good.

WITHOUT A SAFETY NET

I had never known pain quite like it. My legs felt as if they had been staked out in the scorching sun of the Kalahari Desert for a fortnight, resulting in a lifetime's sunburn being concentrated in one single, agonising, blitz. I could feel them throbbing and glowing like a couple of Belisha beacons and it seemed as though they had expanded to about five times their normal size. It was as if someone with a perverse sense of humour had attached a foot-pump to them and jumped up and down on the lever to see how far they would inflate before exploding. I looked up and saw two bewildered faces peering down at me, but the pain was so severe I could hardly speak.

Only seconds before, I had been wandering around the deck of a cargo ship without a care in the world, enjoying the sun and chatting with two Swedish advisers about how well everything was going. Being a great deal more streetwise than me about the dangers that lie in wait on such enormous and busy vessels, it was only to be expected that they would deftly skirt around ropes, wires, pulleys and open cargo holds, whilst I would stumble, trip and fall over every obstacle placed in my path, before tumbling helplessly down a gaping hole that opened up beneath my feet, with little sympathy for my orientation deficiencies, and without warning. When you're a seasoned ship's engineer you keep your wits about you and watch your step. When you're a TV director you look around for artistic and meaningful shots, which means you spend most of your time living in your private dream world and are invariably looking up when you should be looking down.

Now I was suffering the consequences, laying prostrate in the hold and wondering if I was ever going to walk again. It was a small miracle my legs were still in one piece considering I had just crashed onto the sharp metal rim of a large opening with the full weight of my body, causing me to scream out as I plunged into the semi-darkness, and apart from the sheer absurdity of it all, I felt I had let the side down.

I had been sent to Gothenburg by Blackrod a week or so earlier; one of a series of ventures designed to forge a new and exciting alliance with several blue-chip corporations based in Scandinavia. I had so far successfully managed to navigate my way across Holland and Denmark with a British film crew on a number of assignments, the only blip being an unfortunate episode in Amsterdam involving a newly purchased and extremely sharp Swiss army knife that I'd rather not dwell on. And an incident involving an expensive box of blank videotapes that somehow managed to slide off a boat and ended up floating down the Rijnkanaal in an undignified fashion without the faintest hope of retrieval.

But this was something altogether different.

It involved pain and anguish and acute embarrassment and I knew I was about to put a lot of people to a great deal of trouble; people who had far better things to do than winch an imbecile who should have looked where he was going out of a hole. As I was bumped and jostled into a waiting ambulance, I took a final look at the port activity going on around me and realised it had been a losing battle from the moment I had stepped foot on the dockside. Giant cranes hovered menacingly over the skyline as all manner of heavy vehicles manoeuvred about at frightening speed, delivering and collecting spare parts, enormous rolls of paper, cars and massive crates, with no apparent regard for anyone who was stupid enough to get in their way.

And there were added complications. The British crew I had been filming with had left me two or three days earlier because they were booked on another project back in England, so a Swedish crew had taken over. As is often the case, there are distinct advantages in working with locals when you need help sorting out red tape, navigational and geographical problems, guidance on social protocol and etiquette, general access to places and, above all, basic communication. And there are drawbacks.

The Swedish crew had watched in complete bemusement as I was hauled back onto the deck of the ship and were unsure how to react. They had never been in a situation before where they had met the director at the location, briefly discussed the game plan and within a few minutes watched him disappear down a hole, completely disrupting the schedule before it had even begun. In broken sentences, punctuated by pain, I told them to carry on filming and that I would contact them from the hospital after my legs had been X-rayed. Somewhere down the line this message got misinterpreted, because fifteen minutes out of Gothenburg port, Mary, the PA who had accompanied me for moral support, noticed that the crew van was following us through the busy traffic.

After a brief unscheduled stop, during which I explained to my Swedish colleagues that I hadn't meant for them to film me going to hospital but more important background material for the video, Mary and I arrived at the casualty department where two hours elapsed before X-rays were taken and the results known. Fortunately – and by some miracle – my legs were not broken, just badly bruised, but the damage to my reputation had now become a more serious priority as the morphine began to take effect and the ramifications of my stupidity quickly focused my attention. Taking time off to recover was not an option and I needed to get back to the port as soon as possible, despite any misgivings about placing myself back in the danger zone. News filtering back to England that I'd left a foreign crew to their own devices because of my carelessness was something I could not allow to happen. In the freelance world there is no such thing as mitigating circumstances. You can find yourself in the middle of earthquakes, monsoons and outbreaks of civil unrest, but you never return home with excuses. Ultimately the only thing anyone is interested in is: did you get the material? Despite all my skirmishes and flirtations with near disaster in various parts of the world, the answer had always been yes and it was not going to be any different now.

Hobbling about ungainly on crutches I returned to the dockside with Mary, caught up with the film crew and our clients, and completed the filming, albeit in quickly fading Scandinavian light. As it turned out, the setting sun and a sprinkling of unplanned night shots gave an extra dimension to the final Gothenburg scenes, proving that creative lifelines can often be thrown to you when you least expect them.

Any thoughts that I had got away with it, however, were quickly dispelled when I returned to England and viewed the rushes. The infamous Roll 17 contained one or two excellent shots of cranes sweeping across the horizon with their precious cargoes in tow, along with several general establishers of men and machinery in mechanical harmony. These were followed by fifteen minutes of the film director lying prostrate on the deck of a ship, his face creased in agony as a group of ship's crew administered chunks of ice to his legs before strapping him to a stretcher and bundling him into an ambulance. The tracking shots of the ambulance careering along the autobahn were particularly impressive but had no aesthetic merit and I wasted no time in copying off the dozen or so shots I needed for the presentation and dumping the rest of the offending master tape into the nearest bin. When my producer quizzed me about the accident I underplayed it as best I could, dismissing the crutches as a mere precaution. To my horror a batch of photographs arrived on the production manager's desk a few days later which revealed the sordid truth, and would have caused much merriment among the production staff. What's more, they were from our Swedish advisers who had

137

captured the images. In an ultimate act of betrayal, the mischievous twosome had obviously viewed the entire unfortunate episode as vastly amusing, to be re-lived for everyone's masochistic pleasure. Fearing that I would make the front pages of the ITV staff magazine if the photos went walkabout in the office, I spirited the negatives and prints away that evening in a belated effort to preserve my reasonably untarnished reputation, although the many foreign assignments that were to follow did not, in general, always afford me such opportunities to safeguard my dignity.

DRIVEN TO DISTRACTION

It took me a couple of months to fully recover from the accident, and although I was able to dispense with the crutches after the first couple of weeks, I found myself confined to the office writing up project proposals and making short presentations for corporate clients such as Manpower and the British Print Federation. At one point I had the good fortune to work with the actor Anthony Dunstone on a Midland Bank training film and was impressed with his ability to offer up numerous character interpretations, a skill he had perfected through switching between diverse roles in television and on the stage. When we met he was appearing in a play called *The Way of the World*, a comedy of manners written by the English playwright William Congreve. It had originally premiered in early March 1700 and was regarded as one of the best of the Restoration comedies, this version being staged in the West End and featuring Maggie Smith as Lady Wishfort and Christopher Reeve as Millamant. Reeve had shot to prominence in the *Superman* films and whilst he acknowledged the fame and attention that the superhero franchise had brought him, his ambition was to be accepted by the public as a serious actor. I met with him in his dressing room after one of the performances, primarily because I was keen to know if he would be interested in presenting a series I was attempting to get off the ground on the history of magic called *Smoke and Mirrors*. Whilst I had thought the combined imagery of a Master Magician and Superman creating fabulous illusions in their own inimitable fashion might be an interesting visual fusion, Reeve was not entirely convinced. He was more interested in analysing Millamant's character and delving into his psyche, exploring his relationship with the other characters in the play and quizzing me on how I thought the dynamics of the piece worked. I remembered meeting with similar disappointment whilst in New York with Sheldon when we attended the Broadway performance of *Merlin,* featuring the Canadian magician, Doug Henning. Henning was not only a terrific illusionist who had staged some of the most breathtaking magic tricks ever performed in front of a live audience, he had also co-written a biography of Harry Houdini, created illusions for an *Earth, Wind and Fire* tour, and for two of Michael Jackson's concerts, including his 1984 Victory Tour. What he didn't know about magic and magic history wasn't worth knowing but when we called backstage after the show in the hope of being granted an audience, we were told that Henning was too exhausted to entertain visitors and had already left for the night. I suffered a similar setback when I met with the comic Larry Grayson one day for lunch, courtesy of producer Peter Dulay, in the hope of persuading him to put his name to a film script I had written, featuring him as a cabin steward hero of an ill-fated airplane that had crash-landed in the jungle, leaving him to become an unwitting hero, in *The Admiral*

Crichton style, leading the passengers to safety via death-defying ravines, swirling, croc-infested rivers and hostile natives. Larry was flavour of the month at that time, having had a successful TV series, *Shut That Door*, followed by *The Generation Game*. My master plan was to capitalise on this success, assuring him that most of the scenes would be achieved via the magic of visual effects, but Larry turned various shades of white as I pitched the idea to him, looked aghast at Peter when I had finished, then made his excuses and left, his face betraying his horror at the prospect of being plunged into a nightmare scenario that was several light years away from his comfort zone.

Christopher Reeve had at least extended me the courtesy of discussing the possibilities, even though it became evident after our meeting that he did not entirely share my enthusiasm for his role as a caped wizard flying in and out of magic posters and secret cabinets. He was an intelligent, charming man who considered his association with visual trickery to be a means to an end in a world where reality and the merits of personal achievement held far greater significance. I admired him for his honesty in not even offering me a glimmer of hope that he might consider being involved in the project and I returned to my personal reality of training videos and corporate presentations, stuck in rainy London, fearing that I might be deskbound for a good deal longer than was desirable.

From out of nowhere came a directive to go to Switzerland to make a promotion for SAAB - and the chance to wallow in a stimulating new experience surrounded by clean air and blue skies once more. Or so I thought. I should, at this juncture, say on behalf of the many thousands of business travellers who spend countless hours travelling around the world on planes, boats, and trains, that it is not anywhere near as glamorous as it sounds to those anchored in less colourful locations. Not that I'm suggesting it isn't interesting and challenging and educational and life enhancing, completely devoid of frivolous fun and excitement – obviously not, but it can also be stressful, tiring and completely exasperating. For me, Switzerland became a recurring nightmare of traversing yet more precarious mountain roads without safety barriers, but this time with two actors in tow who spent their time bickering and hating every moment of their time together. It doesn't take much for bad vibes to trickle down through the crew and since I didn't have either Andy Parkinson or Sheldon with me to share the pain, I just had to grin and bear it until I was safely back at the hotel each night, where I could indulge in an evening swim and a welcome glass of wine, sitting on a terrace looking out over the glorious backdrop of Lake Brienz and the snow-capped mountains beyond.

It may sound sublime to be in such surroundings but when you are under pressure, have scheduling problems and are coping with fractious working relationships, the days can become endless, especially when you are in a foreign country coping with unfamiliar terrain and communication problems. In those moments the natural beauty and magic of the places you are in can become nothing more than moving back projection. I remember picking up the post one morning a year later and opening a large envelope to find a poster of a stunning hotel looking out over a beautiful lake and breath-taking scenery. 'My God!' I said to my wife, 'We should visit this place some time, it looks amazing!' She took the poster from me and looked it over. 'You idiot, you were there last year, making that film for SAAB.' Which proves that when we become side-tracked we don't always stop to appreciate the wonders around us, even when they are staring us in the face.

Undeterred by the variables that can accost you when filming abroad – most particularly the bad experiences I already had filming cars moving at high speed on unfamiliar foreign roads and mountain tracks – I agreed to take on a new assignment that involved making a title sequence for a series of SEAT training films in Barcelona. Which, naturally, involved four cars travelling at speed on mountain roads, with seven actors who could not speak English, two small children and a dog. I had long since stopped listening to the voice in my head that screamed DON'T DO IT, always convinced that everything just had to run more smoothly the next time round. Jill Roach gave her reassurance that I would be given appropriate back-up every step of the way, even asking Paul Chedlow, our production manager, to accompany us on the recce and shoot. Taking PMs around with you on filming expeditions can be beneficial, but it is not always a good idea. They control the purse strings and can become jittery when a shoot goes off schedule or incurs over-runs, and since the director has the responsibility of making a film worthy of everybody's time and effort, there are naturally moments of disagreement. I have often rejigged a schedule in the middle of filming, having weighed up the immediate consequences and assessed the options for the remainder of the shoot, which may have meant losing a scene or shuffling an earlier one to later in the day. In those circumstances there isn't always time to explain this apparent slip of logic and sudden deviation from an agreed chronology to a colleague who is standing behind you in charge of a limited budget and watching the clock run down.

To his credit, Paul Chedlow was a rock on the Barcelona shoot – although he might not have been quite as understanding of our problems had he not physically been with us. Two weeks of planning in the London office gave no hint of the drama to come, even though Paul, myself and Christopher Cook, the producer, went over everything with a fine toothcomb.

Our first job was to hire a production assistant. We knew from our overseas experience that it is essential to have either a PA or fixer who is local and speaks the language. In London we interviewed a Spanish girl called Monica who had worked for Barcelona TV and displayed no apparent communications difficulties, appearing to speak perfect English. We then arranged to have a Spanish police escort help smooth our passage through the city centre and onward through Catalonia towards Andorra. When your convoy involves four SEAT cars, two crew vans, a minibus carrying actors, animals and children, a client car, and a production vehicle, it's essential not to lose anyone en route, especially since we only had walkie-talkies (no mobiles or SatNavs in those days obviously) with which to control communications. We wanted to leave nothing to chance – but ended up making a fatal error by scheduling the shoot during the Easter holidays, not realising that, a) we would still be filming in the city centre when the entire population of Barcelona was trying to drive back in, and, b) there would be an airport strike bringing serious disruption to everybody's travel plans, including our own.

Unaware of the difficulties that lay ahead and full of optimism that this would be our most successful venture yet, Paul, Christopher and I took a flight to Barcelona so that we could attend a pre-shoot meeting with the client. The storyboard featured four very different car owners driving around Spain in their SEAT cars, comprising a family, a single man, two male business executives and a young couple. The overall effect had to show opulence and desirability. I complicated the storyboard just before we were about to go into the meeting by suggesting to Christopher that we should see the actors in their everyday situations and then place them inside the cars, so that, for example, the business execs would be walking down the street, point to a passing car, followed by an edit to the interior of the car with them now inside in a change of wardrobe and so on. He agreed to present this as an updated storyboard which Walter, the client, agreed to, even though it meant drawing up a revised shooting schedule just three days ahead of filming.

145

Christopher then stayed on in Barcelona to work out schedules for the main training content whilst Paul, Monica and I undertook a recce at the SEAT robotics factory, followed by various locations along the coastal route to Andorra. During the third day, ominous storm clouds began to gather and the wind picked up, so by the time we arrived back in Barcelona, most of Catalonia had taken a near gale-force battering.

But time is money and since we didn't have an endless supply of either, we went ahead with the filming itinerary, despite the fact that two of the crew had been diverted via Rome and Madrid because of the airport strike and didn't catch up with us for two days. At this point we were still filming in the city centre, having incurred numerous problems, not least of which was a technical fault with the camera. Nic Morris wasn't sure how serious it was, and since we were using film and not videotape and couldn't play back the scenes in-camera, we arranged to have the film roll developed in Barcelona so it could be checked before we undertook any more shooting. The rushes were fine as it happened, but that delay, and a further complication with one of the cars breaking down, meant we had not left the city for our first destination as planned. Traffic was starting to build up quickly on the ring roads and was being filtered by our police escort who considered it too dangerous for us to be at the mercy of an endless stream of hot-headed Spanish drivers who were desperate to get home.

At nine o'clock or thereabouts I fell onto my bed, thankful to have at least completed the Barcelona stage of the schedule, with a camera that seemed to be behaving itself and with some excellent scenes in the can.

Day Three, however, did not begin well. Our convoy had spent two hours travelling to a mountainous region where we planned to film an interior car shot with the family, but as we were setting up I saw Monica having a heated argument with the male actor. When I asked what was going on she simply said, 'He is not driving.'

'Yes, he is. The husband is driving the car.'

'No, he can't.'

'He can't drive?'

'No. Nor can the other one.'

'She can't drive either?'

'No.'

I didn't bother to ask if the children could drive. We were probably up shit creek if neither of the adults could drive, and a post-mortem on how Monica had failed to realise the importance of finding actors with at least *that* minimum ability was not going to get us very far halfway up a mountain in soaring temperatures in the middle of a shoot. By good fortune we had a tow bar with us, which meant we could hitch it up to our own vehicle and Nic could film out of the back, with the male actor pretending to drive. But that meant another delay and these unnecessary time-wasting incidents were becoming increasingly frustrating. You allow for some things to go wrong on a shoot but not *everything*.

After lunch we drove back down to sea level to film a car passing by a castle and another around a bend by a harbour. The only problem I had at the

147

second location was a battered old blue van that was parked on the bend exactly where I didn't want it to be.

I called over to Monica. 'Can you go over to where that van is parked and see if you can find the owner?'

'Owner?'

'Yes, the owner of the van. I need him to move it.'

She stared back at me blankly for a few moments as she digested the information. 'We move the van?'

'No, we can't, but if you find the owner we can ask *him* to move the van.'

There was another moment's pause and then her eyes lit up. 'Ah! Si! Si! I understand.'

I smiled with gratitude, pleased that my request had finally got through. She then climbed back inside her car, headed off in the opposite direction and I didn't see her again until later that evening. To this day I have no idea what she thought I had said or how she could have possibly misconstrued the instruction, unless she thought the owner lived in the city and she had gone off in search of him. I filmed the shot anyway, then discarded it in the edit because it was a long way short of visual perfection. When you are promoting a hero car you don't mess up your shot by including a second, less opulent and desirable one.

The final shot of the final day featured a car being driven on a beach by a couple of young, trendy windsurfers. To our dismay the gale force winds that had swept down the coastline forty-eight hours earlier had left some serious damage in their wake. We passed several caravans lying on their side and when

148

we arrived at the beach the sand was no longer solid beneath our feet. Which meant my montage of shots of the car racing along the beach was not going to be as easy as I had thought. I set up the first take, signalled the car to enter shot, and after three seconds watched in dismay as it sank into the sand. Paul observed us struggling to pull the car back onto a firmer part of the beach before hopping back into the production car and driving off with a brief 'Back shortly.'

I had no idea what he had in mind, but the light was starting to fade fast and I began to fear the worst. I asked the windsurfers if they could overnight in a hotel and come back the next morning but they were both scheduled to film a commercial in Madrid the next day, so if we didn't complete the scene that evening, that was that.

Paul returned some twenty minutes later with a tractor and a long length of rope and we spent two hours filming a series of three-second car shots, followed by fifteen minutes of intense towing activity as we pulled them out of the sand. I knew, however, that when all the three-second shots were edited together we could create the illusion that the car was travelling at speed along the beach. My abiding memory of that final day is watching our two policemen friends sitting on a rock, eating sandwiches and watching us with bemused looks on their faces as the sun sank slowly behind them. At least they, and us, could now go home.

When our plane touched down at Heathrow, I thought the nightmare was over – but alas, no. As I passed through the green nothing-to-declare channel a female customs officer scrutinised my passport. 'A television director. Interesting,' which didn't mean, 'let's go and have a cup of tea so you can regale me with all your fascinating stories,' but more along the lines of 'I think we'd better see what you've got packed inside your luggage.' I was, after all, a young, long-haired, media type using his privileged job status as a cover to smuggle in all manner of contraband and illegal substances. She rummaged around in my bags for a few minutes before pulling out the small can of film that I had had processed in Barcelona and holding it up triumphantly. 'Wait here.'

Let me say immediately that customs control at any of our airports do a worthy and thankless job; seldom praised for keeping the country safe, often criticised when criminals or illegal immigrants slip the net. They don't enjoy celebrity status (unless a film crew are making a day-in-the-life of an airport documentary) and they live in a daily climate of suspicion, fear and CCTV, often working long hours with little recognition. But the treatment I received for the next twenty or so minutes at Heathrow was, in my opinion, over the top and entirely unnecessary.

The female officer returned with a young grim-faced man who must have been having a bad day. They marched me into a small, stark, interview room and sat me on a metal chair behind a table. 'You need to know we regard this very seriously.'

Jesus! Had somebody replaced the film inside the can with a bag of cocaine? Surely not!

'What were you doing in Barcelona?'

'Making a training film for SEAT cars.'

'Where were you filming exactly?'

'All over. Most of Catalonia.' I had the worrying thought that maybe Catalonia was a known playground for drugs cartels and money laundering. 'I don't understand. What have I done wrong?'

He didn't answer immediately, just stared at me disapprovingly. 'I have to discuss this with my boss.'

He walked out, leaving me alone in the room with the female officer. I was tired and drained of any energy required to fight my corner with the authorities, the filming and the travelling having put me into an almost zombie-like state of mind.

'I don't know what I've done. Can you tell me?'

'He'll be back soon,' was all she would say. I wondered if it was a ploy to get me to talk; spill the beans of my nefarious activities whilst the grim-faced man observed me on close-circuit TV with his boss.

He kept me waiting a good ten minutes before he came back and sat opposite me again. He pointed to the film can. 'Why didn't you declare this item?'

'I didn't know I had to. We had a technical problem so I had the film processed and put it in my bag afterwards. It's just a roll of film.'

Wrong answer. He looked annoyed. 'It's not just a roll of film. You brought goods of commercial value into the country without declaring them.'

'But this film was listed on the carnet. We took it out of the country and now we're bringing it back in again.'

'What carnet?'

'The one that's with my cameraman.'

'What cameraman?'

'The one going through the red channel showing the appropriate documentation to your colleagues.' At least, I hoped to God that was where he was. If Nic had already passed through and was on his way home I was in serious trouble.

The man grim-faced stood. 'Come with me.'

I followed him out of the room and we walked across to the red channel, in view of the Arrivals Hall, where groups of friends and relatives were waiting to greet passengers who had recently touched down, my wife and children among them. I signalled to her that there was a problem but wasn't able to explain.

'Where's daddy going?' shouted my six-year-old daughter.

'He's been arrested,' said my son, oblivious to my wife's consternation. She placed a hand over his mouth before he could make any further comment.

'What does arrested mean?' I heard my daughter ask as we entered the red zone.

Never had I been so pleased to see a film crew as I was at that moment. Nic was alarmed at first to discover I had been held for questioning, and then somewhat annoyed that I had tucked the roll of film inside my own bag instead of putting it back in the stock box. It seemed pointless explaining that I had just wanted to safeguard the film and not let it out of my sight, but we were all tired and just wanted to get the hell out of there, so I just apologised as the customs officer ticked it off on the carnet and handed the can back to Nic.

But the grim-faced man hadn't finished with me. He marched me back to the green zone, passing my daughter again who shouted 'Daddy! James says you've been arrested! Have you been arrested?' He sat me back down in the chair and read me the riot act, possibly a little disappointed that I had been telling the truth, then began filling in the inevitable paperwork.

'I'm putting you on our blacklist. You and your company. Any breach of regulations on future trips and you'll all be banned.'

It didn't seem fair to tarnish Blackrod with the same brush just because of a moment's naivety on my part and I had the unenviable job of reporting back to my Chief Executive that I had been detained and questioned and that customs would be keeping a watchful eye on the company from now on. Needless to say, Clive wasn't over the moon but could see I was exhausted by the demands of the previous few weeks and concluded it was more of a misunderstanding than an attempt to deceive the authorities. I took some extended leave and slept almost non-stop for about a week, after which I decided it was time to start pacing myself.

ON THIN ICE

When I returned to the office after the Easter break, Sheldon cornered me with a broad grin and announced that we were being reunited for a musical extravaganza called *The Ballantine's Concerto.* I knew that Ballantines was a Scotch whisky of world renown. The concerto part sounded complicated but it had the promise of being something special.

Jill scheduled a meeting that afternoon so we could talk through the proposal. It was a brilliant concept and full of visual energy. There would be five scenarios: a glassblower, an ice-carver, a woman executive, a fashion designer and two skiers, all blended together (whisky distilling terminology) by a small band of musicians who would provide the soundtrack – a feel-good concerto culminating in the glassblower, the ice-carver, the fashion designer, the woman executive and the skiers celebrating their success with glasses of Ballantine's whisky - these final dénouements being revealed at the end of the film. It would look sumptuous and sexy (client terminology) but at the same time informative and inspirational and shaking off the traditional image of old men sipping whisky by the fireside. We were enthused by the concept and couldn't wait to get started.

154

In April 1985, the three of us went into a concentrated research phase as soon as the client had approved the storyboard. David Mindel was hired to score the soundtrack, which we would film to playback in a recording studio later. A fashion designer was then approached to create dresses for a catwalk scene, along with two master craftsmen who would make, respectively, whisky glasses and an ice carving of one of the famous Ballantine's geese, known as The Scotch Watch. This carving would be part of a lavish buffet attended by the designer, the catwalk models and other cast members in the closing scene.

The tricky bit was the ski-ing scenario, because the storyline called for a freestyle skier of the highest calibre. Mike Nemesvary was identified as our number one choice; a young man who had represented both Canada and Great Britain in world events, won three World Cups and three European championships. He had also performed stunts in such films as *A View to a Kill.* We managed to secure his services on condition that we filmed the scenes in La Clusaz, in the Rhone-Alps region in south-eastern France where he was training. I wasn't crazy about travelling abroad so soon after the Barcelona trip but knew it was imperative we featured a world class freestyle expert for Sheldon's proposed 'mountain chase' scenario.

Sheldon was happy to leave the research and filming of the drama scenarios in my hands, but wanted to accompany me to recce the whisky locations which were at the heart of the story. In the summer of 1985, we set off for the Isle of Islay in

Scotland to visit the peat fields and distilleries that would form the central instructional core of the film. The visit, for me, was marked by two distinct incidents. The first involved the flight from the mainland to Islay in a small plane that was buffeted about by turbulence for most of the journey and felt like careering through the sky in a giant milk crate. It was a terrifying experience that left us jaded and nauseous by the time we stepped back onto terra firma. It was a short flight but frankly it could never have been short enough.

The second was our visit to a distillery, where one of the managers invited me to take a sniff into a large wash-back of fermenting liquid. I inhaled deeply, believing it would be a pleasant experience, but reeled backwards as my nose and throat suddenly felt like they had ignited. The distillery man thought it was vastly amusing and rocked about clutching his sides, but I had not had such a painful and disagreeable encounter with chemicals since my first few weeks at Filmatic laboratories. These were ominous omens I hoped would be vanquished by the time we embarked on our long and complex filming schedule.

To be fair, the English side of the shoot went well. Mike Fox was brought in as lighting cameraman for the craft scenes, the female executive, the recording studio and the fashion show, and these looked as visually lavish as we had hoped. It was in La Clusaz that everything began to unravel, mainly due to my lack of experience of filming on snow-covered mountainsides.

The basic scenario involved Mike Nemesvary chasing an attractive girl skier down a mountain, ending with him flying over the edge of a precipice and tumbling poetically through space. The story would end happily with Mike and the girl snuggled up by a fireside in a log cabin drinking Ballantine's whisky. The first scene scheduled to be filmed was the meeting between the two skiers at a cafe lodge situated near the top of the mountain. When we had recced the lodge the sun had been shining, there were very few other skiers around and it looked like the perfect location. Unfortunately, when we turned up to film the next day the skies were grey, the place was buzzing with hundreds of skiers whizzing about all around us and half a dozen snow ploughs were churning up the snow. I abandoned the scene, shuffled it into day two's schedule, and decided we should head over to the log cabin to film the skiers snuggled up by the fireside.

I hoped our luck would improve on day two, but had come to realise that moving people and equipment around on a giant slab of sloping ice is the kind of stuff of which nightmares are made. It is unlikely to turn out to be the quickest, most efficient, or happiest experience unless you can exploit the situation to best advantage. That night I sat down with Mike Nemesvary to work out a gameplan for the following day, which involved filming the cafe meeting, followed by the chase. I had reasoned that going to the lodge first thing in the morning would give us the best chance of shooting without a mob of unwanted noisy extras and machinery in the background, and if we could identify one central filming location halfway up the mountain for the chase scene it would save us a lot of hassle. The fact that it was a high energy pursuit didn't mean we had to place the camera in multiple positions down the entire mountainside. If we could find one central position that offered a changing scenario through 360 degrees, I could shoot several set-ups with different backgrounds and inter-cut close action ski shots with wider shots to create the illusion that they were on different parts of the mountain. It was my only hope of completing on schedule.

Mike knew a couple of possibilities and our chosen location took in a tree line, a row of bushes, a wooded area and a mountain backdrop. Without needing to move the camera more than a few yards for each shot, a dozen scenes were completed inside just two hours the next day and we returned to base a good deal happier.

Which only left the 'tumbling-through-air-freestyle' shot to put in the can. The straightforward part of the shoot. Which it wasn't. As you might have guessed.

To make the required number of freefall tumbles for our purposes, Mike had to launch himself from a curved jump at the end of a steep incline. Because the sun had been blazing down all day, the jump had been slowly melting and by mid-afternoon was not considered safe enough for him to undertake any freefalls. I had to make a call to Jill back in England to tell her that we were unable to complete filming for safety reasons and asked if we could stay over an extra day. To request additional filming time because the sun had come out was weird to say the least but the client agreed to pay for an extra day and filming was completed the next morning after the jump had been given time to freeze overnight. To stand just a few yards from a championship freefall skier as he launches himself into the air, with twists, turns and double somersaults, is, without question, an awesome experience.

I would like to be able to say that the Ballantine's project concluded in happy circumstances but its success as a promotional tool was overshadowed by a tragic accident that occurred not long after we had left La Clusaz. During a routine training session on a trampoline, Mike blacked out during a manoeuvre he had undertaken a thousand times, and landed on his neck. The accident left him a quadriplegic, unable to walk and with no feeling in his hands, at the age of just twenty-four.

He attended the launch of the film at Bafta's Princess Ann theatre, and although he was in good spirits it was heart-breaking to see this talented athlete confined to a wheelchair, knowing that his aspirations to become a supreme world champion would never be fulfilled. In the coming years Mike Nemesvary would re-invent his goals, taking on a demanding Round The World Challenge, driving through four continents and sixteen countries, covering over forty thousand kilometres to raise awareness for spinal cord injury research. He was one of many inspirational human beings I was privileged to meet on my erratic career journey, every one of them giving me cause to think about the uncertainty and fragility of our lives, and to count my blessings.

DOWN TO BUSINESS

By the late eighties, Blackrod had been trawling in more work than its staff contingent could handle, so freelancers were drafted in to help meet deadlines. Since broadcast productions were not considered to be a core part of the company's output, most resources were poured into developing and nurturing the corporate client base. That isn't to say broadcast TV was no longer on the agenda. The formation of Channel 4 in 1982 had offered new opportunities to independent programme makers who had not been able to find ways of penetrating the established inner sanctums of either the BBC or ITV. Channel 4 gave them a voice; a diversity of viewpoints and freedom of creative interpretation; a channel that extended viewers' choices, encouraged innovation and made programmes of special appeal, to both the mass market and minority audiences.

Although Blackrod had not been awarded a broadcast commission since *The Spice of Life,* Jill and Michael had invested a great deal of time considering ideas that were relevant and different for terrestrial television. They were enthused by the idea of producing a show targeted at the small business community; a series of programmes committed to helping entrepreneurs who were prepared to take risks in order to establish a successful and profitable enterprise, and to that end worked up a proposal outlining their objectives.

The Business Exchange, a live programme with pre-edited video inserts, was commissioned by Channel 4 in 1986 and put us back into broadcast production. Jill Roach produced the series and sent me on the road to film several of the mini documentary inserts featuring both successful business achievers and budding entrepreneurs who were in need of advice from the programme's panel of experts in the studio. This gave me a chance to sharpen up my interviewing skills, asking questions that needed to be searching and succinct, but without upsetting anyone. One highly successful businesswoman who had built up her own company from scratch, and whose name I discreetly withhold for reasons that will become apparent, was first on my list for interview. She arrived promptly for the session in her boardroom, exactly to the minute, hair styled to perfection, her expensive suit giving an immediate declaration of her status as a woman not to be messed with. She sat down in front of the camera, expressed her wish that the interview might be conducted within fifteen minutes as she had an important meeting to attend, and waved her hand by way of saying, 'so let's get on with it.'

I shuffled my notes about, hoping she might eventually shed her Ice Queen demeanour so that a warmer, friendlier persona might emerge for the viewers to empathise with.

I cleared my throat. 'Can I start by asking if you always had ambitions to be a successful businesswoman?'

She considered the question for a few moments and then offered the following words of wisdom: 'I believe all successful people are driven. They have a strong desire for success, even from an early age. I remember as a child always wanting to be better and smarter than the other children in the neighbourhood, which often alienated me. I was an only child, so I spent most of my time playing with myself.'

She stopped, realising what she had said, exclaimed 'Oh shit!' and started laughing. It was our cue to join in and share her moment of mirth as we attempted to put such a vivid and voyeuristic image to the backs of our minds. It was near to impossible and several attempts at a restart reduced us to even more tears. We took a five-minute break so we could pull ourselves together and when we started over I relegated the question to the back of the list and began by asking what inspired her to start her own company. The rest of the interview flowed better than I could have dared hope; she was perfectly relaxed, answered each question with a reassuring smile and gave full, complete and knowledgeable answers. When we wrapped at the location, I was relieved that I had enough material to make an interesting programme segment. For many years after, when called upon to conduct an on-camera interview, I would recall that moment when the ice was broken - and the difference it made. Never again would I underestimate the difficulties of eliciting information from people and the importance of establishing mutual understanding and respect before you put them in the hot seat.

All the subjects we filmed for the show were unique and inspirational in their quest for success. Karen McCloud, a small but feisty twenty-six-year old from Glasgow, had set up her own business customising motor bikes despite resistance from the local male biker community, many of whom found it difficult entrusting their machines to a woman. She spoke openly on camera about the problems of running such an enterprise single-handedly, accompanied by shots of her hammering, sawing and welding late into the night, as she effectively sacrificed her private life in pursuit of her dream. Thankfully, over the next few years she would win over her male detractors and build a successful customer base.

Bob Payton, an American restaurateur and former advertising executive, had introduced the brands Chicago Pizza Pie Factory, Chicago Rib Shack and Henry J Bean's Bar and Grill to London, but had deeper ambitions to live in the style of the English landed gentry. To that end he purchased Stapleford Park, a mansion house surrounded by five hundred acres of Capability Brown landscaped grounds nestling in the heart of England near Melton Mowbray. I filmed sequences showing some of the restoration work being undertaken on the building, along with some scenic pastoral shots of Bob galloping through the grounds on his horse so they could be intercut with busy lunchtime scenes at one of his London restaurants. He was larger and life, had big ambitions, and was proud to be immersing himself into English country life. Sadly, those dreams ended in July 1994 when his car went off the road near Stevenage and he was killed outright, aged just fifty. Stapleford Park today stands as a testament to his desire to create somewhere special for patrons to relax and enjoy the finer things in life that had brought him so much personal pleasure.

The Business Exchange was a brilliant concept but the show failed to gain the audience reach it deserved, due in no small measure to its unfortunate Sunday morning slot, and was subsequently dropped. Although the series had a short life span, it was, for me, a massive learning curve as it made me more conscious of the perils and pitfalls involved in starting a business – and introduced me, at first hand, to the excitement of multi-camera studio recording, even if initially as an observer.

Studio direction requires a different set of disciplines from single-camera directing, because the camera shots are chosen and edited in real-time rather than being selected and assembled in an edit suite after recording is completed when you have time to reassess your options. This requires total concentration, since mis-timed camera cuts and bad on-screen co-ordination can look messy, and when you don't have an option for retakes – during a live show for example – the end result can look embarrassingly unprofessional. Despite having worked for three years at Thames TV's studios in Teddington I had no experience of studio direction but it completely fascinated me, made all the more adrenaline-pumping observing from the gallery on *The Business Exchange* as phone calls came in from viewers and Jill shouted instructions into Michael

Rodd's earpiece. His reactions were always cool and measured, giving no hint of the manic voice screaming in his ear, and despite all the things that could have gone pear-shaped during transmission, every show ran like clockwork.

It occurred to me that no director's CV would be complete without multi-camera skills on the list so I persuaded Clive to let me take a leave of absence to work on London Weekend Television's live *The Six O'Clock Show* so that I could accumulate more experience of the mechanics of studio recording. The show was fronted by Michael Aspel and featured Danny Baker, a comedy writer and journalist, Fred Housego, an ex-cabbie who had won the *Mastermind* competition, and Paula Yates, a flamboyant and eccentric TV presenter and writer who, off-screen, exuded a child-like innocence. Paula was destined to have a troubled life, culminating in a shock revelation by a journalist in 1997 that she was the secret daughter of Hughie Green. She died from an accidental drug overdose just three years later. Listening to the playful banter between her and Fred in the studio gallery at London Weekend Television back in 1987 - he likened her to a luminous blancmange when she sat next to us wearing a bubblegum pink dress – nobody could have predicted that such a spirited, fun-loving, woman would meet such an untimely and tragic end.

The show itself, a genial mix of information and entertainment, had suited her on-screen personality perfectly. Unlike *The Business Exchange*, *The Six O'Clock Show* had acquired an enviable Friday evening transmission slot due in no small part to its

165

general appeal and the chemistry of the presenters, with healthy viewing figures that had been growing steadily.

Magazine in format and running at a breakneck half an hour, the show told stories of London life as captured by a small team of presenters roaming around the capital with a camera crew in tow. My first baptism of fire was a story involving two pizza establishments that were at loggerheads, aptly entitled *War and Pizza*. One of the pizza parlours had been trading for a year or so but was starting to lose custom to a new enterprise that had set up just a few doors down, copying their rival's menu design and menu list. The conflict wasn't quite as bad as I had feared as both parties took it all in good spirit, aided and abetted by the presenter, Fred Housego. His light-hearted approach made for entertaining viewing, given comic support by the various marketing tricks the two pizza owners used to attract custom, including a suitably attired Superman handing out 'flyers'. It was one of many stories I covered over the years that gave me cause to wonder after how things worked out for the people we filmed once the camera crews had packed up and left; whether life for them carried on as normal, or if our presence influenced any future decision-making process. Fifteen minutes of fame often seem important to so many - although perhaps not something a young and ambitious TV director should give himself sleepless nights worrying about when there were other, more pressing, concerns to be addressed in a growing period of uncertainty.

I had seen the writing on the wall for two or three months. As the eighties gave way to the nineties, there were several significant events that shaped the future of the television industry and my own destiny.

In November 1990 Prime Minister Margaret Thatcher resigned, but not before sealing the fate of the broadcasting unions, which she had described in her own words as the last bastion of union power. By the time she left Downing Street she had achieved her objective; the ACTT was just weeks away from being dissolved, having sounded its own death knell some months before, with BETA and NATTKE, who jointly represented workers in most areas of cinema, television and video, amalgamating to form BECTU. The new organisation now had diminished clout, due to the loss of the closed shop, technological change, industry fragmentation, frustrated hostile management, and a growing but less controllable freelance market. By the end of the eighties, money was not so abundant and there were growing fears of recession.

Not surprising that in such a climate, corporations were no longer investing as heavily in promotional videos or inter-company training and communications initiatives, which meant Blackrod had to fight its corner in competition with an increasing number of production companies who were prepared to lower their margins in order to secure commissions.

Clive Moffatt left Blackrod in 1988, after which the company went through numerous management changes and amalgamations, firstly with Chrysalis Television, then First Information Group, who both retained the Blackrod brand, and finally a merger between Michael Rodd and Rob Lipfriend that would become Lipfriend Rodd International. Just two years later TV South lost its licence to Meridian Broadcasting, marking the end of an extraordinary period in my chequered career.

My recollections of Blackrod's ultimate demise are, at best, hazy. My eight years with the company had been amazing; working with producers like Jill Roach and Michael Rodd who gave me extraordinary opportunities to write, direct and travel the world; to develop my skills in virtually every area of a changing technological landscape and to appreciate just how lucky I was to be able to sustain ongoing employment through difficult times in a fiercely competitive market place.

I was fortunate to be able to continue working with Michael on many of his post-Blackrod projects, though I was genuinely sorry to see Clive leave. He had been amazingly supportive; a good-natured, well-meaning executive of tremendous integrity, and I'm pleased that his company, Moffatt Associates, has grown and prospered since.

Whilst the projects we undertook as a team at Clipstone Street were hugely successful in the main, I can't help thinking that just the one transmission for *The Spice of Life* series on Channel 4 is something of a travesty. Thirteen half hour programmes on the history of herbs and spices, filmed throughout the world by a team of first-class directors and cameramen, showing meals being prepared, cooked and enjoyed in an African outback, at a Maharajah's banquet, and a plush New York hotel, with narration

168

by Edward Woodward, scripts by Sheldon Greenberg and music by Carl Davis – who wouldn't want to see that today?

Yet it's likely that nobody actually knows where the transmission masters are anymore, or who owns the rights after all these years of change, takeovers and managerial reshuffles. That such an extraordinary creative enterprise celebrating world culture and tradition should have become so easily discarded, or lost, is a monumental oversight.

That aside, the Blackrod years were joyous and rewarding and I will always cherish the memories of my time with them.

NEW DIRECTIONS

As the Blackrod era drew to a close, many of the producers I had worked with left to join independent companies who were pitching ideas to potential clients in an effort to win contracts and establish ongoing relationships. Money was tight, so it was essential to present workable formats that were not only full of creative vigour and imagination, but also met the client's communications criteria. More importantly, they had to be achievable within the time scale and come in on budget. This invariably meant that directors had to continue to be inventive and resourceful but with less time and money available to them.

Since independent production houses had no desire to take unnecessary risks, there was a high demand for directors who had a track record in fulfilling client briefs whilst working under pressure. I felt it might be wise to capitalise on this philosophy before that experience was eventually (and predictably) usurped by cheaper alternatives (self-shooting camera operators/directors for one) so I invested some time in re-establishing working relationships with ex colleagues at Blackrod who were now winning some interesting commissions.

The first of these was Maureen McCue, who had now taken the helm at Rank Film Training, a production house that was investing in making training dramas for sale to a wide range of companies within the UK, a marketing initiative that Video Arts, John Cleese's company, had already turned its hand to very successfully. The gameplan was simple but effective and took a different approach to the accepted business practice.

It was customary for a client to request a film or video production that would serve a particular purpose relevant to that company's needs or objectives. Many large corporations devised training programmes and communications strategies tailored to a specific business model. They believed they had something unique to offer their staff and customers, and as such, the pitches from producers needed to address these specific objectives.

Rank Film Training decided there was also a market for more generic requirements within organisations and devised and produced a whole raft of videos that were relevant to the needs of the majority of potential clients, whatever their individual working practices. It also made financial sense. If a company commissioned a bespoke fifteen-minute video presentation using a professional camera operator, writer, director and actors it might cost them in the region of, say, £20,000 to £30,000. It would be more cost effective if they could buy, or rent, off the shelf, for say, £1,000, a video that covered all their relevant requirements; a fraction of the outlay. Therefore, if Rank Film Training made a film for £20,000 and sold it on to 200 companies, it would give them a healthy return and a greatly increased profit margin. Rank took the initial risk with their investment, but if they got it right the dividends would justify the outlay. And Rank, like Video Arts, consistently got it right.

The first presentation that Maureen asked me to direct was a film about theft in the workplace. It was irrelevant whether that workplace was a local newsagent, a factory or three floors of open plan offices. In most situations employees were not aware of the procedures in the event of theft and how such a crime impacted on the management, the staff and those who were culpable. Using actors, we filmed a scenario involving two employees at a factory who were spiriting away merchandise, one involving small items, the other much larger. The film gave an insight into how to spot a potential theft, how to deal with it, and the ramifications. We even created a courtroom in a studio, complete with a judge and jury, to illustrate how serious the consequences of theft can be. The film was an immediate success and became a valuable educational tool for numerous businesses across the UK.

Professional actors featured regularly in many of these corporate training films because it was essential that managers, employees and members of the public were represented on screen as characters that appeared credible and could gain empathy with the viewing audience. Richard Standeven, a director who had worked on an impressive array of television dramas, once told me that you had to love actors to be able to work with them effectively. There is no question that professional performers are worth their weight in gold, but as I had discovered from the Olivier experience, they can also be sensitive and insecure, in need of regular praise and encouragement. I was far too manipulative and technically focused on creating good continuity flow and strong dramatic edit points to give actors the time and freedom they deserved. I didn't have the patience and have to concede that even though those I worked with gave excellent performances, it was clear to me early on that making quality drama was not going to be my forte because my handling of actors was unintentionally ham-fisted and insensitive. Even at auditions I would invariably say something that would be misrepresented or misunderstood. Like telling an actress role-playing a shoplifter that she had expressively shifty eyes which made her perfect for the role. Or the actor who, when auditioning for the part of a lorry driver, asked me what his motivation was after reading through his four lines of script and I told him he needed to be very articulated. He wasn't in the least bit amused and rightly so. Actors and extras often have to pay their own travel expenses to attend auditions and expect to be treated with the utmost respect for their time and effort. Fortunately, my lorry driver was the perfect choice and I was pleased to offer him the part. It taught me, however, to tread more carefully if there was the remotest chance my remarks might cause offence or backfire. Generally I found it too demanding to give my full attention to actors when I was trying to complete a fractious filming schedule, particularly on foreign shoots when the pressure reached boiling point. That said, most actors and performers have been a joy to work with, not just because of their professionalism but the patience and generosity they showed toward both me and their fellow performers, and I'm indebted to them for making those experiences rewarding and fun.

My second film for Rank Film Training was a complicated scenario which brought me, not for the first time, dangerously close to the kind of perilous environments that are out of my personal comfort zone, if not forbidden territory. *Waiting to Happen* was a twenty-minute presentation showing how easily accidents can happen in a factory environment and the steps needed to be taken to avoid them. Maureen was keen for me to research and write the script, so I arranged a meeting with a Health and Safety Executive to help me devise a matrix of circumstance to cover off most of the possibilities. The first point he made was that there is generally more than one cause of an accident, disasters often resulting from a build-up of negligent practices from different departments, over a period of time. This provided an opportunity for me to construct the narrative like a detective mystery.

The starting point for our discussion involved a fork-lift truck veering off course, crashing into a ladder and knocking off a welder who was spot-welding a metal grid, his blow torch landing just a few feet from a pile of flammable materials – so we worked backwards from there. In the final script the first conclusion drawn by the on-screen investigation team is that the fork-lift truck driver is to blame for the accident – but as the story unfolds we reveal that a visitor to the factory has been allowed to wander away unsupervised from the main party, inadvertently stepping over a badly faded yellow safety line, causing the driver to swerve a fork-lift that was in need of a service, over an oil patch that had not been cleaned up, into a ladder that that was not marked with a red sticker as unsafe, nor secured to the grid, the blow torch landing next to the combustible materials that should have been taken away a day or so earlier. The final number of contributing factors to the accident totalled more than twenty, making the point that everyone employed in a factory has a responsibility to be vigilant and to report any possible breach of safety regulations.

The film hit the mark with factories up and down the country, enabling management to persuade their staff to become more safety conscious at a fraction of the price it would have cost for a tailor-made video or film commission. In hindsight it is hard to believe that I took on such a project, considering my aversion to industrial locations that contain moving fork-lift trucks, conveyor belts, welding torches, explosives and heavy machinery. By a miracle I emerged without as much as a scratch, so for those of you who may have been anticipating that considering my horrific experience in Gothenburg, at the very least I would be hit by a fork-lift truck on day two, stumble into the ladder and consequently be squashed by the welder as he landed on top of me, may be disappointed – perhaps cheated - that such disaster never materialised. Most of my next ventures were not quite as trouble free, however, as, against my better judgement I was exposed to varying degrees of discomfort and anxiety, all in the honest pursuit of making a living.

When the Corporation of the City of London decided they wanted to update an earlier film presentation they had made extolling the wonders of the city in order to attract foreign investors, I found myself attending script sessions in large intimidating meeting rooms at The Guildhall, discussing filming possibilities across a finely polished oak table with a select gathering of counsellors and advisers, and sitting in a padded leather high-back chair with the City of London crest emblazoned across the headrest. No T-shirt and jeans were an acceptable part of the dress code in this historic emporium, which oozed tradition from every painting, beam and chandelier. As with many corporate productions, a large number of interested parties were keen to put in their two-penny worth and it took four or five meetings, with various changes of client personnel, before the structure of the film was finally agreed.

The Corporation's previous film was hopelessly out of date, the opening shot showing an army of bowler-hatted bankers swarming over Westminster Bridge as a male voice-over announced: 'The City of London, where men go to do business.' Such a statement was unthinkable in 1990, so it was important to correct the balance. I created a storyline in which a young female photographer wandered around the city taking pictures, referring occasionally to her guide book – a visual device that allowed us to use her voice track to give the viewer relevant information about the Corporation's 800-year history and its many functions as a local authority. This meant filming a wide range of scenes on the financial trading floors, in the parks, out and about with the police (including a high-speed chase that threw us around in the back seat of a patrol car like rag dolls), and numerous activities that came under the Corporation's extensive umbrella. Day One involved a helicopter shoot over the city, which I embarked on hesitantly since I still had vivid memories of my aerial tour of the Highlands. Added to which it was stifling hot and London itself was covered in a blanket of cranes and scaffolding. It was difficult to capture scenic shots that did not include towering metal winches and grappling hooks and it became increasingly difficult to show London as the picture postcard place that visitors would readily flock to. To the casual observer it might even have seemed the City was falling apart. We were also required to film various Corporation functions that illustrated the pomp and ceremony associated with one of the world's foremost capitals, including a scene with the Lord Mayor entertaining an overseas dignitary – which meant travelling between locations all over London, under a hot, unforgiving sun, wearing a jacket, shirt and tie.

It had not been the easiest of projects to bring to fruition because too many decisions had been made by committee and in those circumstances editorial control often becomes a sticking point. It is often difficult to persuade a client not to present vast chunks of information that an audience cannot digest, or retain, when a strong creative interpretation of the objectives can perform the task so much better. The completed film did fulfil the brief, however, and as far as I know helped to maintain the City's position as a centre of financial excellence. If we were making the same film today the main objective would probably be to restore confidence in the various financial institutions that had tarnished their reputation with accusations of fraud, deceit and greed. I doubt if even Houdini would be able to pull that one off.

After my city adventure I dipped in and out of the weird and the wonderful, each project throwing me a curve ball whenever my back was turned. Like the Midland Bank film that involved a naked male presenter, complete with bath cap, sitting in a bathtub full of water and bubbles to illustrate how pension fund profits were topped up via the taps, whilst the withdrawals disappeared down the plughole at varying intervals. It was all extremely silly, and the presenter (whose name I withhold to save him any undue embarrassment) had problems giving us the required information without laughing himself silly or soaking the microphone, compounded by an intermittent problem with the filler pipe that resulted in two overflows on the studio floor, and the crew skidding about trying to stay upright. When the video was finished, I contacted another ex-Blackrod colleague, Roberta Aarons, to see if she had anything in the pipeline that didn't involve helicopter flights, manic car chases, bubbles or bathtubs, and was pleased to be offered a project with her company, Jacaranda, for the Royal Automobile Association. The RAC was undergoing a change of image and wanted to unveil its new logos and business strategy to its staff as soon as possible, so it was all hands to the pumps for an immediate turnaround. The RAC headquarters were strategically positioned along the M5 motorway just outside of Bristol and I discovered that videos were being made there on such a regular basis that neither the staff nor management were in the least bit phased by having a camera and microphone suddenly thrust in their faces.

After an initial meeting with the board of directors in London to go over the filming schedule, I set off to the West Country to experience at first hand just why the RAC claimed to be the elite in roadside assistance. To my dismay there was a loud clunk from inside the bonnet of my car, followed by a spectacular hiss of steam, forcing me to take remedial action and swerve across three lanes of the M4 in a cloud of smoke and up an embankment. By a sublime twist of fate an AA patrol vehicle travelling half a mile behind had seen me meander off the motorway and stopped to help. Shortly after I found myself being towed into the RAC car park by an AA patrolman who clearly enjoyed the irony of it all. But there was worse to come.

A few weeks later I left the edit suite in London with the editor and my client, Mike Betts, after a late-night session. The three of us had jammed ourselves inside a small lift and were making our way to the ground floor accompanied by a dozen bags of rubbish that had been piled up in the corner by the cleaners, when the lift juddered to a halt between the third and second floors. Thankfully we had cell phones and could summon help, but the memory of spending forty-five minutes in a cramped, smelly lift cage waiting to be rescued and then having to watch a respected client clamber halfway up a lift shaft in a neatly pressed suit and being hauled out the other end by the fire brigade is an image I would prefer to forget. It was time for a change of direction and it came from an unexpected quarter.

A GIANT TRAIN SET

The one significant reality about working in television is that all experience is good experience. Learning from mistakes and capitalising on your acquired knowledge is essential if you want to progress – and that means keeping an open mind on opportunities as they present themselves. I had not had any involvement with children's television since my spell on *Magpie* with Thames Television some twenty-three years earlier, yet now it seemed the perfect genre for me to be able to apply my accumulated skills in documentary, current affairs, drama, light entertainment and comedy. Satellite broadcasting was beginning to establish itself as a contender alongside the traditional terrestrial channels and for me this presented a chance to get to grips with multi-camera direction and explore unchartered territory. This came courtesy of The Children's Channel, one of several specialised channels set up by a consortium of Thorn EMI, Thames TV and British Telecom, with Richard Wolfe the channel's Chief Executive, and Dan Maddicott, who had previously worked at Longman Video, its Director of Programmes.

The channel had started life in the mid-eighties, initially for cable subscribers but later transmitting via the Astra satellite. These two broadcasting outlets were still very much in their infancy, treading new ground in terms of structure, politics, organisation and programme output. Budgets were not overly generous, particularly as the audience reach was significantly smaller than the established broadcasters and many channels were sharing their cable and satellite air time. Apart from such shows as *Jack in the Box*, presented by Carol Chell, and *Roustabout,* presented by Mick Robertson, The Children's Channel's early output relied heavily on acquisitions – programmes that were bought in from other countries – but by early 1990 TCC was making many of its own programmes and was commissioned by the newly formed British Satellite Broadcasting to use this experience to make an entertainment show, *Hold the Pickle*, produced by Michael Forte and featuring Lee Evans and Rebecca Front, along with a location series, *Sportsbag.*

I had discussed various possibilities at The Children's Channel a year or so earlier, but with only a three-day week on offer due to limited budgets and a slender production slate, I'd had little choice but to decline the opportunity to beat a path back into the world of children's TV. But with British Satellite Broadcasting entering the fray in October 1990 with an injection of money to pay for these two new series to complement the established puppet shows, cartoons and magazine formats, Dan was now able to offer me a contract on *Sportsbag* that was more attractive, both financially and creatively.

I was pleased to be working with such a young and enthusiastic team, and became fired up with renewed motivation. It was a lucky break that would propel me into a magic kingdom full of invention, and equip me with new skills I could never have acquired without the technical revolution that heralded the arrival of space age television.

The excitement of those first few weeks, however, was almost scuppered halfway through filming due to a quickly changing broadcast landscape that was to have sudden and dramatic consequences. At the time there were two main giants in the arena competing to dominate the satellite revolution, British Satellite Broadcasting and Sky Television. A confrontation was looming between BSB, initially anticipated as the UK's only satellite service, and Murdoch's Sky, which was mounting an aggressive drive to control satellite transmissions in the UK.

I was, of course, blissfully unaware of this sabre-rattling when I embarked on the initial planning stages of *Sportsbag*, focused as I was on extending my skills and making a series of programmes that would hopefully showcase my abilities. Helping me in this endeavor was the presenter Fiona Farrell and a wonderfully dedicated researcher called Alice, both of whom accompanied me on the location recces. The schedule was ridiculously tight; our task was to recce two locations in a single day – invariably in the same vicinity to cut down on technical set-up and travel time – spend the following day planning the shoots and writing the scripts, then return to the locations on the third day, complete with a small scanner unit and three camera operators, to tape two fifteen-minute shows, one in the morning and one in the afternoon, after which I would return to London the same evening to edit both shows for transmission the following day. Under normal circumstances I would have dismissed this timetable as completely unachievable, but I knew it was the chance of a lifetime and I had the support of a team who were incredibly dedicated, including Robb Hart, TCC's technical wizard, who assured me he had worked out a failsafe system to smooth the production's passage.

It only took us a couple of shows to get into our stride, thanks in the main to Fiona's ability to relate instantly to the on-screen contributors and understand the techniques of any of the sports that were thrown into the mix. The format was relatively straightforward: a guest sports personality outlined the rules of the chosen sport to the viewers, then gave tutoring sessions to teams of schoolchildren, followed by some Top Tips, these assorted contents topped and tailed by colourful animated graphics and some up-tempo music. The biggest challenge technically was to set up in two completely different locations on the same day in order to cover the two contrasting sports, one possibly water-based, another on grass or in a gym. Because I was vision-mixing between the three cameras in real time - save for one or two pre-planned tape stops – it meant that when I returned to London for the evening edits, I simply had to glue together the pre-edited elements and insert the graphics and music.

Most of the shows ran smoothly, with many traditional sports being covered along with some new ones - plus inspirational input from the guest sports personalities, including the judo Olympic coach Roy Inman, American basketball player Alton Byrd and cricketing legend Trevor Bailey, who gave an excellent tutorial on the techniques of soft-ball cricket.

Others didn't go quite as planned.

We had covered off the majority of potential problems at the planning stages, from technical hitches due to rough terrain or bad weather, from illness to accidents, but the unpredictable was always standing by waiting to mug us. With little room for error within the time scale, I had decided to walk through each segment of the shows with Fiona, the guest personality and the kids, and then return to the scanner to record the takes. The only time this went awry - and almost sank us - was during filming of the yachting programme, which featured Fiona battling with an unruly sail whilst receiving instructions from an expert in a small craft that bobbed and weaved its way around a large lake at Cranleigh. The recce had already alerted me to the fact that the cameras would need to be as mobile as possible in order to keep up with the craft and that positioning them around the lake on dry land would produce an undesirably static end result. Without realising just how precarious the alternative would be, I sent one cameraman off in a dinghy whilst I accompanied another in a small boat, complete with a megaphone and battery-operated monitor so that I could check the shots as we filmed them. The two hours we spent attempting to record a ten-minute item reminded me of the recce problems I had encountered in Catalonia a few years earlier, when a heavy wind that had been absent on the recce suddenly conspired to make the task near to impossible on the shoot day.

In such conditions it was not only difficult to choreograph the shots, but with so much noise from water spray, whistling wind and flapping sail, I couldn't hear a single word of the dialogue between Fiona and the expert and had to play each take back through headphones so that I could decide if the recordings were usable. Having almost fallen in the lake and taken some very expensive kit with me on a couple of occasions, I ditched this approach for the third hour by putting one of the cameramen on board the yacht itself, but the cramped conditions and continual need for everyone to keep ducking in order to avoid being knocked unconscious by a sail that swiveled manically over their heads, made it unacceptably dangerous.

I abandoned Plan B and initiated Plan C, which involved recording the main instruction sequence on dry land, with simulated sail movements so that the sequence could be edited later with the handful of usable shots taken on the lake itself and some general cutaways taken by the onboard cameraman, all of which would be linked seamlessly by the instructional voice track. Fiona felt we ought to film at least a couple of shots of her sailing one of the smaller craft on her own, which gave us some excellent bonus footage until the vessel capsized, leaving a drenched and bedraggled presenter clinging on for dear life.

It was another lesson in ensuring you have back-up plans in place *before* you turn up for filming rather than having to continually think your way out of trouble. This episode of unpredictability was, however, a mere prelude to a filming day the following week that turned out to be the ultimate location nightmare.

On this particular morning, we had set off under an increasingly ominous sky, having been given the news that *Sportsbag* was to be cancelled and there would be no further filming assignments. British Satellite Broadcasting and Murdoch's Sky Television, having struggled with the burden of huge losses, escalating debts and ongoing start-up costs, suddenly announced a merger; the formation of a single company, operating as British Sky Broadcasting (BSkyB) but marketed as Sky. The merger saved Sky financially as it had very few major advertisers at the time, so acquiring BSB's healthier advertising contracts and equipment helped to solve the company's problems. It meant, however that there would have to be extensive restructuring, with revised programme schedules, in which event the majority of current productions would now be axed.

I didn't have time to evaluate what this meant for The Children's Channel, or for me, as we had a tough filming day ahead of us, made more complicated by the fact that the first show featured diving in the pool at the National Sports Centre at Crystal Palace, with the second item, football, being filmed on a nearby playing field that had been taking a complete drenching throughout the morning and had turned into a quagmire. I just hoped the rain would ease up by the time we needed to record the football tutorial and concentrated on talking through the diving format with Fiona and organizing the camera positions. Watching my technical supervisor run electricity cables around the slippery perimeter of such a vast area of water did little to alleviate my anxiety and I resolved to beat a hasty retreat back to the scanner once we were set and ready to go.

Apart from the familiar wall of noisy, echoey sound associated with indoor pools, the voice tracks we recorded were surprisingly clean and the item was filmed inside an hour without any of the equipment being drenched, or any of the camera operators being electrocuted. We were able to break for an early lunch and took the opportunity to reset the scanner by the side of the playing field without the usual race against the clock.

Then came the bad news.

The office rang to say that Bobby Charlton, who was due to join us for the afternoon session, had withdrawn due to business commitments and was sending someone to take his place. Charlton, one of the World Cup wining side of 1966 and a footballing icon, had created The Bobby Charlton Soccer and Sports Academy in 1978, a prestigious soccer training school that was responsible for nurturing the talents of many of the country's professional footballers including, in 1987, a young David Beckham. Having Bobby Charlton feature on *Sportsbag* would have been one of the highlights of the series so there was massive disappointment that he had withdrawn. On top of which it was still raining and I now had to go and tell a group of over-excited twelve to fourteen-year-old boys who were kicking a ball around boisterously in the mud that Bobby Charlton would not be coming and that someone else would be taking the session.

'Well who is it then?' asked one. 'Is it Gary Lineker?'

'Or Gazza. Is it Gazza? shouted another hopefully.

'I don't know, lads, we haven't been told. It'll be as much as a surprise for me as it will be for you.'

Ten minutes later I stood outside the scanner and watched as a car drew up in the car park and a young blonde girl in her early twenties stepped out. She was wearing a pair of spotlessly clean white shorts, white T-shirt, white socks and trainers and looked every bit like a rep for a soap powder company. I waited with baited breath as she bounced up to the scanner and introduced herself with a beaming smile. 'Hi, I'm Pat. Bobby Charlton sent me.'

I smiled in return, hoping not to betray my reservations about how the afternoon might pan out now that I had two sporty females standing by to give a group of wound-up schoolboys lessons in improving their football skills. I left Pat with Fiona to chat over the basic gameplan and returned to the pitch, hoping my news wouldn't spark a riot. Their reaction was only to be expected.

'She's a *girl*. We ain't playing with girls!'

'Yeah!' screamed another, 'football's a *boy's* game!'

There were echoes of Bill Forsyth's 1981 film *Gregory's Girl*, in which Dee Hepburn turns up on a playing field in her fetching blue and white kit to lend her footballing skills to a hapless boys' team, ousting John Gordon Sinclair from his position as striker and winning over the rest of the lads with her impressive skills.

My lads were not quite so accommodating. There was a general chorus of disapproval, followed by a unified show of resentment as the boys peeled off and ran amuck, kicking the ball wildly in all directions and stamping in the muddy puddles. I failed at any attempts to reason with them until their teacher came to the rescue and rounded them up by one of the goalposts and reminded them they were going to be on national television and that they would be letting both themselves and their school down if they didn't co-operate.

'But girls can't play football!' insisted one of the lads, regarding me with a massive sulk.

'What do *they* know?' chimed a second.

I could have told them that women's football had been played in England for over a century, was very popular and acknowledged as becoming a true rival to the men's game. I might have mentioned that a Preston ladies team playing at Goodison Park as far back as 1920 attracted a crowd of 53,000 with another 15,000 turned away because the ground was full. I might have pointed out that many of the UK football league clubs had a women's team and that the national side had been playing on the world stage since 1972. Had I been in possession of a crystal ball I could even have told them that the national squad would qualify for the FIFA Women's World Cup four times, reaching the quarter final stage on each occasion in 1995, 2007 and 2011, winning Bronze medals at the semi-finals in Canada in 2015, and would reach the semi-finals of the Euros in 2017 and the World Cup in France in 2019. But I doubt it would have cut any ice. They were a bunch of angry young men who were expecting to meet one of their heroes and were now hell bent on being as disruptive as they could. Whilst I understood their disappointment, I had a show to produce under the most trying of circumstances and could only plead with them to show respect to a woman whose skills Bobby himself obviously had a high regard for. They agreed to give her the benefit of the doubt but despite the fact that Pat really did have a natural aptitude for ball control and tactics, they found it difficult to take her seriously and did their utmost to sabotage the session without being too obvious. So when Pat arranged for one of them to take a free kick and placed herself in a favourable position inside the penalty area, shouting: 'Okay, lads, on my head, let me have it,' they duly obliged.

Thwack! The ball hit her forehead with such ferocity it left a large muddy imprint and knocked her backwards, after which she more or less set herself up as a sitting target every time she organized a set piece. By the time she trudged wearily back to her car two hours later she was covered in mud from head to foot with hardly an inch of white showing. To her credit she took it all in good humour, having doubtless been just as uneasy about giving advice as the lads were in taking it. Thankfully I had filmed enough material to edit the item down to an entertaining and instructive fifteen minutes, aided and abetted by a couple of music montage sections which would hopefully give no hint of how difficult it had all been, though we were mighty relieved when it was time to pack up the kit and head back to town.

I had assumed that the demise of *Sportsbag* would signal an early departure for me from The Children's Channel, but by now Central Television and publishers DC Thomson & Co had joined the consortium and with increased advertising revenue there were some interesting projects on the in-house production slate. First up was *Comic Cuts,* a straightforward and inexpensive studio magazine show that had already been in production for a few weeks. It was produced by Mike Barfield, a comedy writer who had worked on numerous radio shows, including *The News Huddlines,* starring comedian Roy Hudd. Mike was also a respected cartoonist and comic enthusiast and the show gave viewers an insight into the fascinating world of popular British comics, including *The Beano, The Dandy, Topper and The Eagle,* with their iconic characters such as Roger the Dodger, Minnie the Minx and The Bash Street Kids. Recorded at Teddington Lock in the same studio where *Magpie* had been made more than two decades earlier, *Comic Cuts* was written and researched by Mike, who selected the on-screen graphics with the help of graphics designer Bob Jobling, and co-presented the show with illustrator Chris White. *Comic Cuts* incorporated mock interviews with a range of comic strip characters, including Roy of the Rovers and Dan Dare, with caption competitions, drawing masterclasses and cartoon inserts. Like much of TCC's output it was a low-budget show that deserved a much wider audience and was a good example of how to produce an engaging children's show on very little money.

Hot on its tail came a location programme, *On The Road*, a single-camera shoot rather than an OB, involving a director, cameraman, PA and the presenter, Gareth 'Gaz Top' Jones, who had already fronted one of TCC's popular studio based shows. The idea was simple: we would travel the UK filming short items of interest, covering subjects as diverse as sport, history and theme parks, each show lasting ten minutes. Most of the items had been researched and set up in advance, but with TCC always looking to fill air time with inexpensive material, we needed to keep our eyes and ears open for any event that might be worth covering 'on the hoof.'

Fortunately, Gareth's cheeky, friendly persona allowed him to persuade almost anyone to either appear on camera or give us permission to film on their property, so we were able to conjure up several items that were not on the original hit list. He also had an extraordinary retentive memory which enabled him to scan through research notes just before a take and then reel them off on camera as if he were an expert on the featured subject. Thus we filmed items at historical landmarks, theme parks, festivals and exhibitions, Gareth making the items both fun and informative. He also had a genuine enthusiasm for the stories, along with a real affection for children. On one occasion I watched him help a small boy whose model airplane had crashed into a tree, happy to spend his entire lunch break piecing it back together for him until it was airborne again.

Gareth also used his immense charm and passion to ensure that that any of the stories we filmed went several stages further than many presenters might have been prepared to go. Our day in a themed Wild West town, for example, was made all the more interesting when he took part in a High Noon shoot-out in the main street and then persuaded the manager of the Golden Nugget saloon to let him accompany two of the can-can dancers inside a stagecoach that was to be attacked by a bunch of renegade Red Indians in a spectacular presentation in the public arena. It gave me an opportunity to film a fast-paced item that would intercut between hostile Indians on horseback, the cowboys who were chasing them, and Gareth being jostled around inside a stagecoach, accompanied by two sassy dancers who thought the whole thing was an absolute riot. He also volunteered to hold a piece of paper at arm's length whilst a whip-cracking cowboy demolished it in five super-fast strikes, the last of which almost took Gareth's fingers off and left him reeling in a fair degree of pain. Undeterred, he was keen to take part in a jousting contest at the Camelot Theme Park, a notion I managed to talk him out of on the grounds that it would probably signal an early exit for both our careers, his being infinitely more permanent than mine.

Our final few days were spent in Bristol, where we filmed an item from the Clifton Suspension Bridge about its designer, Isambard Kingdom Brunel, followed by a backstage tour around the Bristol Old Vic, a trip on a private yacht, and finally a visit to the Bristol Balloon Festival, a yearly event that attracts thousands of visitors, not all of whom are fortunate enough to cadge a lift in these inflatable miracles of flight. My private ambition to sweep majestically over the skies of Britain standing inside a wicker basket, listening to the occasional roar of an onboard flame, was scuppered when I realised that there would only be enough room for the balloon operator, Gareth, Paul Cudjoe the cameraman and Simon the sound recordist. Since they were more than capable of filming the item without my input, I waved them off after a quick briefing, a little disappointed to have missed out on the opportunity, but determined to try it at some time in the future, which of course I never did.

We rounded off the series with some magnificent aerial views of Bristol and the various locations we had visited, along with an informative commentary from Gareth, and some tips from the expert on how to fly and navigate a hot air balloon. The series was well received and for me became the launch-pad for some ground-breaking TCC projects, made all the more fun to work on with the support of such a dedicated team. Chris Evans, who had yet to make his mark as a highly popular and intuitive TV presenter, took part in a celebrity edition of my next Children's Channel venture, *The Super Mario Challenge.* Super Mario was one of the most popular computer games of the early nineties, so addictive that Nintendo were keen to sponsor the television version which featured two teams of children pitting their skills against each other. Chris participated with his trademark anarchic gusto and is one of a handful of people, along with the likes of Michael Aspel, Michael Portillo and Michael Rodd, who are able to stay cool, on air, under pressure, whatever mayhem is going on around them; the kind of broadcasters that any less

195

experienced presenter would be lucky to have by their side during a live transmission. The show could have followed the predictable and accepted path of children's game shows, but with Robb Hart devising the format, it was never going to be that straightforward.

Robb had started at The Children's Channel in the mid-eighties, charged with the task of getting the channel on air technically, with a range of responsibilities from studio direction to the censorship of bought-in cartoons, which involved having to remove potentially offensive sections, including beheadings from the cute Japanese cartoon series *Choppy and the Princess.* After a brief spell away with MTV Europe, Robb had returned to TCC in 1988 as Head of Production, working closely with Dan Maddicott devising shows that would make full use of advanced broadcast technology. Robb brought in Maria Djurkovic to design the studio set and asked me to direct. It was a complete act of faith on his part, because although I had now begun developing my multi-camera skills on *Sportsbag, The Super Mario Challenge* was a different kettle of fish altogether, involving chromakey, split-screens and composite overlays, all happening in real time.

I decided not to be intimidated by the complexity of it all and took up the challenge, knowing that Robb would be in attendance throughout the recordings to oversee their technical execution – and that to turn it down would be to relinquish my hard-fought position as series director at the channel to someone else. Freelance television directors are, by their nature, territorial animals, marking out their boundaries like cats and dogs and staking their claim to productions to the exclusion, if possible, of all others. Apart from which, *The Super Mario Challenge* promised to be particularly challenging.

The first task was to chat over the floor plans for the studio set with Maria and Robb. It soon became evident that for *Super Mario* we had to have a 360-degree set, which meant any cameras that were cross-shooting would be seen in vision. Whilst this was a perfectly acceptable technique for certain talk shows and concerts, the Super Mario world had to be an abstract place where magical things happened, and studio cameras would have been an intrusion. Maria - who would go on to production design such cinema classics as *Billy Elliot, Sliding Doors, Mamma Mia!* and *Tinker, Tailor, Soldier Spy* - came up with the idea of hiding two of the camera lenses behind the black spots on the Super Mario wooden cut-out mushrooms, with a third positioned behind a large screen that we would overlay in the final edit with computer feeds of the games in progress, and a fourth camouflaged in black behind the studio audience. It worked well, due in no small measure to the knowledgeable Mario supremo John Lenahan, who presented the show in full cartoon costume, with Robb supervising the layers of visual effects. John, an American illusionist, corporate entertainer and former title holder of Street Magician of the Year, had been resident in the UK since 1984 and knew the intricacies of Mario gameplay backwards, so he was the perfect choice.

As with all TCC shows, we recorded several back to back, with quick turnarounds for props and team members in between tape stops. Since *The Super Mario Challenge* happened in real time, we were able to complete twelve fifteen-minute shows a day, enabling us to stay ahead of our transmission slots.

Turning up for work every day was like walking into Hamleys toy store and making for the model train set, with its diverse collection of trains and multi-coloured carriages. I could run them on tracks that took off in all directions and involve them in all manner of wondrous adventures, with spectacular changes of scenery and numerous surprises waiting around every bend. But if I had thought *The Super Mario Challenge* was multi-layered, it was a mere test run to the project that Dan and Robb had tucked up their sleeves and were particularly excited about.

Dennis the Menace had started life in *The Beano* in March 1951, its stories of a mischievous schoolboy who had a knack of attracting trouble eventually becoming its longest running comic strip. DC Thomson & Co, *The Beano* publishers, had decided it was time to bring Dennis and his trusty sidekick Gnasher the dog to life on our television screens and The Children's Channel was charged with the responsibility of creating a vehicle for the characters that would reflect the design and humour of the comic itself. Robb persuaded an old art school pal, John Bonner, to return from the US to design the comic strip background worlds with the help of Bob Jobling, and set puppeteers Mike Quinn and Dave Barclay of Ultimate Animates to work creating the puppets. Quinn and Barclay's credentials included *Star Wars, Little Shop of Horrors* and *Fraggle Rock*, so they

198

were perfectly placed to bring the Dennis characters to the small screen. Mike Barfield was immediately engaged to write the scripts and I came on board as series producer/director.

At a production meeting we went over the delivery schedule. Mike would write a hundred or so storylines for approval by DC Thomson, then convert them into scripts so that I could rough out basic drawings to show John Bonner my visualisations for the action. John would then convert the drawings - be they fields, streets, school playgrounds, bedrooms or garden sheds - into professionally drawn coloured backgrounds that mirrored the designs in the comic, as requested by DC Thomson. These graphics would then be delivered to the studio the following morning on videotape so that we could incorporate them into the shows, as backgrounds behind the puppets, who would act out their roles against a green screen. This technique, known as chromakey compositing, is used for layering two images or video streams together, replacing the green background from one, with an image from the other. Thus, Superman can fly through the air on wires that have been 'painted out' on a blue or green backround that is subsequently replaced with moving background images of the camera weaving in and out of buildings or through clouds.

It all sounded fairly straightforward but with limited time and on a small budget, it turned out to be a heady challenge, and there were unforeseen complications.

When Mike and Dave unveiled the Dennis puppet for the first time it was a work of art and reflected a perfect, spitting image of Dennis the Menace. But he had rodded hands, and although this was a standard method of operation for many puppet shows, Dennis was an all-action character who should be able to run, ride on roller-skates and skateboards, tumble through the air, fire catapults, and pick up various objects and throw them in all directions. None of which could be achieved without actual operational hands and legs. One answer would have been to simplify the scripts but the action would not have replicated the energy of the comic strips, so Ultimate Animates agreed to rethink how he could become more animated. Whilst they headed back to the drawing board, John Bonner raised the question of how the bubble captions were going to work. These were the comic bubbles that contained words like SPLAT! or SPLODGE! at moments when some yucky mixture smacked into walls, cupboards or fences, or PONG! whenever Dennis let off one of his customary stink bombs. Robb came up with a solution that was ahead of its time and involved the use of laser discs. John would create the bubble words, animate them and transfer them to laser disc so that they could be activated instantly at the appropriate moment during recording. The idea excited John so much that he began complicating the art work, despite the time constraints, by adding animation to most of the backgrounds. It was a good example of how ideas can grow organically when a production team is fired up.

With Mike's scripts now coming at us in a landslide of ingenuity, Dan Maddicott and I undertook read-throughs on every script, checking both dialogue and action in order to address any possible problems that might arise during the recordings. Logan Murray, the stand-up comic, was then contracted to voice all of the characters, including some virtuoso dog-type grunts for Gnasher, and these pre-recorded voice tracks were sent to the studio for the puppeteers to mime to. Robb had taken the decision not to post-edit the shows after the recordings, which meant we had to record as 'live' in a small, makeshift studio in a basement in Wardour Street and end the day with completed shows ready for transmission the following morning. The monitor bank in front of me showed three studio cameras with the characters against green screen: one on a standard long shot and the other two for cross-cutting on the puppets' faces. Three other monitors showed the corresponding graphic backgrounds that John and Bob had supplied for insertion behind each of the studio shots, each change of shot showing the characters in front of a different background, depending on the required frame size and geographical position. A seventh monitor displayed the animations on the laser disc and an eighth monitor the main composite shot comprising the puppets with their combined backgrounds. The composites switched accordingly as we cut from shot to shot but a further complication arose at the end of each scene when we had to initiate a pre-planned tape stop or stop recording because of a technical problem. Because we had no edit time, the VT operator had to wind back the tape and run it forward again so that when we reached the stop point, recording re-commenced in real time with, hopefully, an invisible edit. This meant running in the voice tracks at the exact same point, with the puppeteers on standby, ready to pick up the action, either where it had left off or at the beginning of a new scene. By a miracle most pick-up points were inserted seamlessly, with picture and sound in perfect synch, thanks to the patience and professionalism of the technical staff and the puppeteers.

The experience showed me just how much I did not know or understand about puppeteering. I was walking into a room full of hidden trapdoors and falling down every one of them. On one occasion, when Walter the Softy was fighting his way out of a paper bag, I asked Geoff Felix, the Walter puppeteer, on open mike, if he could see okay out of the bag. There was a stunned silence, broken by a slightly bemused floor manager replying over the intercom: 'But Bob, he's not actually *inside* the bag.' One of the cameras panned round to confirm that Geoff was standing below the platform performance area, holding the paper bag in his hand and looking confused by my comment. It was the first of many moments when I wanted the floor to open and swallow me up, though thankfully the puppeteers thought this naivety amusing; perhaps even a compliment to their skills in making me believe that Geoff really *was* concealed inside the paper bag.

They weren't always so forgiving, though for the most part they were very patient; waiting for various pennies to drop as I got to grips with a form of programme making that was completely alien to me and that I knew would take time to master. Because the puppeteering community is incredibly guarded about their techniques and working methods, it would take me another decade before I would be able to converse with them at an acceptable level of unified understanding and make my own suggestions as to how certain complex routines and visual tricks could be achieved. For now, despite the complications of the special FX, *The Dennis the Menace and Gnasher Show* became one of The Children's Channel's biggest successes.

Putting that accomplishment into context, however, the show's audience share at the time could never compete with the terrestrial channels, and it was disappointing that such an innovative series, made on limited resources with great care and passion by everyone involved, would only be seen by a minority audience. Robb Hart had, however, pulled out all the technical stops and Mike Barfield somehow managed to create single-handedly over a hundred very funny scripts within a manic time frame, for which he deserves a place in the Scriptwriters' Hall of Fame.

Dennis the Menace marked the end of my time at The Children's Channel. Ominous clouds had begun to gather again over the blue sky of opportunity, conspiring to spoil the party and pull the magic carpet from under me; the usual round of inter-company politics and reshuffles that occasionally rocked the boat within TV companies and constantly reminded me just how precarious the freelance life can be. By 1992 Dan had decided to leave the channel to take up a new role as Controller of Children's and Entertainment at HTV in Bristol, part of the ITV network. Since I didn't care much for the kind of programmes that might now roll off the production line at TCC I decided it was time to call it a day and leave the train set for others to play with.

Just a few months later, Robb Hart left to take up a position with Virgin Atlantic in California, making computer games that incorporated A-list movie stars. He soon adopted Los Angeles as his permanent home, where he lives today, running his own production company and making blue chip commercials and presentations with his individual brand of visual sorcery. With both Dan and Robb out of the picture it was unlikely I would have enjoyed the same creative freedom at the channel, the same chance to experiment and develop new programme ideas, to enjoy the kind of camaraderie that had existed with the production staff. It was a sad but inevitable end to a wonderful adventure but between us we had developed the knack of making something out of nothing; hours of entertaining and informative children's television on a shoestring, and I had enjoyed every minute of it.

TRIAL RUNS

The next three years proved to be difficult as work eventually trickled to a standstill. I moved the family to Suffolk to escape the stresses and strains of living in the London area, hoping that a change of environment might help to improve the quality of our lives as well as giving me a chance to re-assess my career objectives. The downside was that I could no longer hop on a tube or taxi if a sudden job was on offer in the capital, and commuting between Suffolk and London on a daily basis was not an option I would have seriously entertained, even if the transport links had worked efficiently.

I had hoped to pick up freelance work at Anglia Television, but with a clutch of established directors already on the payroll it didn't look promising. Anglia's cache of seasoned directors had not been wasting time marking out their territory simply to relinquish their ground to an interloper from London, apart from which the nineties were ushering in a new era of austerity within the broadcasting sector that was to have serious ramifications on jobs and production output. Already programmes were being trimmed back at all the ITV regional stations, with many permanent staff finding themselves out of work and given no option but to freelance on temporary contracts. When I first came to Anglia Television as an assistant editor some thirty-eight years earlier it had been a thriving, bustling community of technicians producing a wide range of programmes, from documentaries and magazine shows of local interest, to game shows, plays and dramas transmitted over the network, including *Sale of the Century, Bygones, Survival* and *Tales of the Unexpected.*

Looking back, it doesn't seem possible that such an industrious broadcasting institution would eventually go into decline. Anglia's launch in October 1959 must have been a moment of euphoria for those who lived in the region and were involved in its early days of production; long-term, secure, employment; creative challenges working on programmes of local interest as well as network shows, with the added bonus of being in the heart of the countryside, operating independently away from the Big Smoke.

By the early part of the new millennium, following numerous takeovers and acquisitions, Anglia Television would occupy very little of its original space in the historic Agricultural Hall in the centre of Norwich, with its production output whittled down to just news coverage, transforming it into a mere shell of the formidable organisation it once was.

Little of this was evident in 1993 when I began submitting programme ideas to the producers at Anglia, who politely rejected my project outlines, even though, curiously, many of these formats subsequently appeared as internally produced productions at Channel 4 and the BBC, broadcasters who clearly did see their potential. A brief chink of light came with an offer from Tim Child at

Broadsword, whose company was based in Norwich making the high-rating children's studio show *Knightmare*. Tim was interested in my involvement in special effects shows such as *Super Mario* and *The Dennis the Menace Show* and felt my input might be useful. He had started filming a new show on location in the East Anglia region called *Timebusters,* as well as supervising the pre-production phase of *Virtually Impossible*, a studio game show that had yet to be piloted.

My first recording day as director on one of the *Timebusters* series might also have been renamed Nightmare. The show involved two actor/presenters travelling through the Cosmos in an old London bus, along with two teams of contestants, one kitted out in yellow, the other in red. When the bus touched down at a suitable location - on this occasion Somerleyton Hall in Suffolk - the teams had to head off in search of a sealed document that would reopen the Time Vortex and allow them to take off again. As with *Knightmare,* the youngsters interacted with actors in costume whilst they were puzzle-solving, and there were numerous filming techniques employed, from dramatic set pieces, cabled multi-camera set-ups that I could keep track of from inside the scanner, to single camera hand-held mobile scenes that I had little control over, since the action was widely spread over several acres between the two teams of contestants. The schedule was close to manic. Kids and cameras were whizzing off in all directions in a cosmic blur, looking for the vital document, taking part in off-the-hoof drama scenarios in tunnels, mazes and drawing rooms, with the scenes tied together by special effects links which Tim had a complete handle on at any given time but the rest of us did not. Whilst I accepted that it was not always possible to predict what was going to happen next because of the nature of the gameplay, I felt that one or two clues of possibility would have been useful, a problem compounded by the fact that he would suddenly dream up a new filming scenario out of the blue that had to be immediately accommodated.

In short, a long-term working relationship between Tim and myself was never going to be on the cards; he was completely focused on controlling the geographical flow of the action and unlikely to entertain any meaningful creative collaboration with a third party within the time scale he was working to.

That said, Tim Child is one of the true geniuses of televisual conceptualisation, a man ahead of his time. His ideas and attention to detail were truly innovative, with new technological boundaries being rewritten at every turn, on shows that illustrated his uniquely fertile imagination. It is one of my regrets that we did not bond in the way I had initially hoped and therefore never had an opportunity to explore where any kind of collaborative head-banging might have taken us.

For my Broadsword swan song, I directed Tim's studio pilot for *Virtually Impossible* but it was a stressful day, made all the more difficult working with a crew who had been informed of cuts in production personnel, and were de-motivated as a consequence. I withdrew from being involved in any further *Timebusters* episodes, or any of the *Virtually*

Impossible series, and took time out to reconsider my game plan.

There were limited options. In early 1995 freelance work had come to a standstill during the dismal, barren months of February and March, traditionally a time when the broadcasters' Christmas deadlines have been met and everyone is waiting to see what new projects might emerge from hibernation as spring approached.

When the phone eventually rang it was Dan Maddicott, who, in his new role as Controller of Children's and Entertainment at HTV had been developing a number of new programme ideas with the ITV Network Centre. It had been two years since Dan and I had enjoyed a creative liaison, so I was interested to hear that he had won a contract to produce a series based on his own creation, *The Slow Norris*.

Slow Norris is a giant sloth who lives in a damp cave and eats delicacies such as slugs and snails, and befriends a small girl called Allie who teaches him about the world around them. Dan had read these stories to his daughter, Buddy, when she was younger, so he had already enjoyed the benefit of a test run with the target age group. Now they were to be brought to life in a specially constructed set at HTV and Dan invited me down to Bristol to discuss the possibility of my taking on the role of producer/director. It all seemed perfectly straightforward: four puppets interacting in a studio to themed stories that mixed education with playful fun, regular 'on location' inserts, but little in the way of special effects.

Except that when I sat down at a meeting with the puppeteers and the designer, Deborah O'Boyle, it soon became evident that we would be working our way through a creative obstacle course. The challenge was to create fifteen shows of fifteen minutes duration based around a six-foot sloth, a three-foot child, and a worm and a beetle whose maximum height averaged two inches, all four characters very often interacting within the same set-up. Moreover, the Slow Norris costume was to be made in America from a specialised bear-like material consisting of real fur to give added authenticity. It would be extremely heavy and the head section would have to be removed at half hourly intervals to avoid any risk of the puppeteer inside expiring in such a hot and claustrophobic environment. An added problem was that Slow Norris's eyes had to be unusually large, cartoon-like, and operated electronically off set. Which meant the puppeteer playing Slow Norris would effectively be acting out his role 'blind' on a platform five feet off the ground, surrounded by the four foot 'trenches' that allowed the Allie puppeteer to move freely up and down the set.

Ultimate Animates had been contracted to build the puppets, with David Barclay playing Slow Norris, and Mike Quinn operating Ally and Walter Worm, aided and abetted by Karen Prell and Helena Smee. The problem of David working blind on the platform was to be solved by the introduction of a small monitor inside the head section through which the live pictures would be displayed to him. I worried that the amount of sweat and condensation generated inside the head-piece might affect the electronics, but the puppeteers assured me that the possibility of any short-circuiting was unlikely as they had used a similar system before. Relieved that David's eyelids would not melt, or his hair ignite, I was left with the problem of how to film four characters with such varying height differences within the same scenario. It was decided that Mike and David would build miniatures of Walter Worm and Ben Beetle that could be seen in the master shots, but filmed from behind so that their inability to 'talk' would not be apparent. Larger, puppet-sized, fully operational versions of Ben and Walter would then be recorded later so that the segments could be edited into the master shots in post-production.

For Deborah this meant constructing a giant sub-set which mimicked the main set, including changing weather conditions to reflect the four seasons, and giant props such as apple cores, matchboxes, twigs and leaves, to match the originals. It was going to be a mother of a continuity exercise, since every interaction involving the larger puppet versions of Ben and Walter would have to be shot *after* the main scenes involving the miniatures had been recorded for all of the shows, matching head movements, eyelines and Michael Lingard's intricate lighting set-ups.

I agreed to go away and work out a system that could accommodate this master plan, whilst Deborah drew up designs and floor plans for both studio sets, and Dan sent the first thirteen story outlines to writer Jeanne Willis. Jeanne was an established author who had previously worked for a number of advertising agencies creating press adverts, cinema, radio and television commercials, and characters including the Sugar Puffs Honey Monster. Her impressive back catalogue of best-selling books included *The Monster Bed* and *Dr Xargle* and she was the perfect choice to bring Dan's storylines to life on the small screen.

I returned to Bristol a few weeks later for a read-through of the draft scripts with Dan; he taking the role of Slow Norris and Ben Beetle, and me Allie and Walter Worm. The readings helped us to time the shows and get a feel for the character interactions. They also focused our minds on what was possible and what was not within the limitations of the filming and the puppetry. I had already discovered from working on *Dennis the Menace* that a writer's bountiful imagination did not always correlate with the practicalities of studio recording when time is of the essence. Jeanne had an instinctive feel for all of the characters' dialogue and the set pieces were not only funny but played at two levels: one aimed at the children and the other at the adults watching with them. I just needed to tweak the stage directions, in particular the integration of the Walter and Ben sub-set, to ensure that the action would appear seamless on screen.

In one show, *Things That Fly*, The Slow Norris flies a kite but loses control of it as Walter Worm gets tangled up in the string and becomes airborne. In the same show, Walter, complete with aviator helmet and goggles, climbs into a miniature aeroplane and whizzes around the set before crash-landing in a pond. It was immediately apparent that a second reading of the scripts would be required for such an intricate manoeuvre, involving the puppeteers and Deborah, to ensure that we could iron out how the visuals would work without causing severe hold-ups and expensive head-scratching on the studio recording days.

The scripts and visuals taken care of, we turned our attention to the sound. Musician John Du Prez (who later co-wrote the music for the Monty Python musical *Spamalot*) was contracted to compose songs and musical links, with Nick Ryan voicing The Slow Norris, eight-year-old Buddy Maddicott voicing Allie and the versatile Gary Martin applying his exceptional skills to voicing Ben and Walter. I was keen to record the voice tracks in the traditional manner of radio shows. I knew that many animated feature films were voiced by well-known cinema actors at individual recording sessions without the other actors necessarily being present, but this was more a matter of convenience due to their various global filming commitments. We did not have that problem so it meant I could sit our voice artistes around a table in a sound booth so that they were able to read the scripts as a collective; sometimes amending them when suggestions were made that would improve the interaction.

Once the music was recorded - many of the songs featuring Norris, Walter, Ben and Allie - I would spend time with a sound editor pacing the voices and music so that we ended up with a complete sound track running exactly to time that could be played back to the puppeteers in the studio during the final recording. It was a failsafe system I was to use on every future show I produced that involved puppets.

There is no doubt in my mind that the greatest investment anyone can make in a production is prep time. When a director turns up for work either at a location or in a multi-camera studio he or she will invariably spend, if they're lucky, about ten per cent of their energy being creative and ninety per cent resolving issues that materialise on the day. So if you haven't planned accordingly, heavy compromises may have to be made. I have observed directors wing it on filming days, some successfully, others less so, but whilst directing by the seat of your pants may be a stimulating experience for some, I was never inclined to put my reputation on the line unnecessarily. For each of the fifteen shows I drew up detailed floor plans showing the movement of the puppets and their corresponding camera positions and included sketches showing all the eyelines. The intricacies of the shoot were then discussed with first AD John Parris, who had the difficult job of co-ordinating the movement of puppets and cameras on the studio floor as dictated by the plans. By the time we assembled at the studio for the first shoot day few stones had been left unturned, so all we had to do was record the scenes chronologically, with Shirley Lock, my PA, marking down the time-codes for each master shot so that we could call them up later and match the action when the time came to shoot Ben and Walter on the sub-set, something that would not have been possible without a video playback facility.

David, as expected, had to be extracted from his Norris costume at regular intervals to take in oxygen and cool down, the soggy suit being hung up overnight to dry. There was one unfortunate episode when the studio had been locked up for the night and the water spraying from David's after-show shower in his Winnebago turned ice cold and he was left dripping wet, in the cold, clutching a towel around his midriff. It marked the beginning of a fraught relationship between HTV and Ultimate Animates that was to have regrettable consequences in the months ahead.

A COLD WIND FROM THE EAST

A few weeks before the first series of *The Slow Norris* was transmitted, I had been bombarding the London-based broadcasters with programme ideas that could be filmed in the East Anglia region, giving me the dual benefit of making a network series but filming it and post-producing it in the area where I now lived. It was not a game plan that had immediate success, but I knew the satellite stations were hungry for well made, low cost, product. After three or four months of blitzing fifty or sixty producers and executives, I received a letter in early August from Liz Barron at The Learning Channel, saying she was interested in some of my hobby format ideas. I had intended to pitch half a dozen concepts to her at our initial meeting but decided to throw all my eggs into one basket and outline my idea for a series targeted at the theatre world.

I had discovered there were scores of books written about the art and craft of theatre, but virtually no videos available that offered on-screen advice about acting, make-up, set design, stage managing and prop-making. I knew that professional practitioners' on-screen interview fees alone would be expensive, not to mention royalties on copyrighted works. Liz could see the potential in utilising amateur dramatics groups to illustrate, at low cost, the various areas of theatrical production. I knew of numerous amdram groups who performed plays from their own scripts, designed their own props and even composed their own music, and as long they gave us blanket permission to transmit their work, a thirteen-part series could be brought in well below the normal cost for six and a half hours of screen time.

Liz almost commissioned *Stagestruck* on the spot, but first I had to devise thirteen programme formats, with themes, and links, and make contact with any professional actors, directors and designers I knew who would be prepared to take part in instructional workshops for fees that would not blow my budget. It took three weeks of planning, during which I made umpteen telephone calls to any contacts I felt I might have a chance of persuading to come on board. Then, having drawn up thirteen programme outlines, I was ready to offer contracts to, among others, Richard Martin the acclaimed television and theatre director, Ian Westbrook, an eminent theatre designer, Andrew Killian, a highly regarded stage manager, and Christina Barryk, a young but experienced actress, to take part in the series. I had worked with Christina on several corporate and training videos and felt she would be perfect as the series presenter, having a warm and friendly persona as well as a strong track record in both television and theatre.

Having agreed with the contract department at The Learning Channel that *Stagestruck* would be made under my own company name of Spellcaster (which effectively landed me with both the risk and responsibility for the budget and schedule), I visited scores of amateur dramatics groups throughout East

217

Anglia on a mission to find a rich and varied mix of practitioners, as well as some interesting characters to interview and tell anecdotes on camera. The first filming date of November 14th was agreed, individual performance contracts sent out to a hundred or so participants, and I was poised to go into pre-production.

And then a spanner fell into the works. A very large spanner. Of industrial proportions.

I received a call from the production manager at Sunset and Vine, who were making a series to celebrate the forthcoming Olympics in Atlanta, called *Olympic Hall of Fame*. We had discussed the possibility of my directing one of the programmes several months earlier, but since it was purely speculative at that time, I had not considered it a serious proposition. Now here she was, informing me that an agreement had been made with Vasily Alexeyev, the Olympic weightlifter, to film his story in Russia, and was I available to take up a short-term contract?

It created an immediate dilemma.

I had, on many occasions, spent days on end twiddling my thumbs, willing the phone to ring, only to find myself suddenly compromised by being offered filming schedules that might collide and leave an embarrassing aftermath, dumping me squarely in the mire. On this occasion I had signed a contract that committed me to taking full responsibility, through Spellcaster, for delivery of the *Stagestruck* series to TLC by mid-December, ready for a New Year transmission.

I had limited time to make a decision because my passport was required so that a visa could be arranged, and I needed to speak with the fixer in Moscow to talk through a possible filming schedule. There was no point trying to take on the Russian project behind Liz Barron's back, so I contacted her and explained the situation. She was pragmatic and pulled no punches. I had signed a contract and was aware of the *Stagestruck* delivery dates. Any failure to comply with these dates would have consequences, but how I deployed my time outside of our agreed scheduled commitments was entirely down to me.

I sat down and pulled out my diary to see if there was any possibility I could take on both projects. Working back from my first TLC filming date of November 14th, I realised I only had three weeks in which to submit a completed budget, schedule and script to Liz for final approval of the *Stagestruck* series - and organise a workable filming schedule in Russia. It was tight - and there was a lot at stake if everything went pear-shaped. Like my entire career. A pre-filming recce in Russia wasn't a possibility because of time and money constraints, which eased the pressure on the pre-production phase, but under normal circumstances it is never wise *not* to pre-visit locations ahead of filming.

The trip to Moscow was earmarked for mid-October, around the start of the Russian winter (average temperatures -20°), involving five days of filming and travel, returning in the last week of October for a week's editing. Which would leave me with just two weeks to make final preparations before *Stagestruck* went into production. It was a gamble.

Ironically, I would be playing Russian roulette with my future. Only an idiot would subject themselves to such folly.

So I agreed to go to Moscow and film the Vasily Alexeyev story, unable to resist this once-in-a-lifetime opportunity and confident I could meet all my deadlines without stressing myself and everybody else. But if I had thought that all my previous trips abroad were plagued by seemingly insurmountable difficulties, Russia was about to take the biscuit big time.

Sunset and Vine sent me tapes of two of the completed shows profiling Olympians Mark Spitz and Sebastian Coe so that I could see how the format worked. It was all very celebratory as one might expect: upbringing, childhood ambitions, sporting achievements and current activities, mixing interviews of the selected sporting heroes and their trainers with appropriate archive footage and music. Homage to success and athleticism at the highest level. With limited knowledge about Alexeyev I needed to contact the fixer, Olga, so that we could identify possible filming locations. There wouldn't be time to stand around figuring out what to film once we hit Moscow and the clock started ticking, so the more prep we managed long distance the better. Olga spoke excellent English and was excited that we were going to Russia to meet one of her heroes. I told her I needed to film some visually interesting scenes in Alexeyev's home town of Shakhty; possibly set up a family gathering to include his wife and two sons and their families. She came back to me after a couple of days saying a get-together was arranged and suggested we might consider filming Alexeyev visiting a gym in Shakhty where the local boys practiced their weightlifting. She also told me Alexeyev had made his living working down the mines prior to his success, and should she arrange a reunion with some of his former colleagues at the pit head? It took little more than a week to put everything in place, including appointments at the Moscow Archives, where we needed to select and purchase the library footage.

So far so good. And my visa arrived on time, so it was all systems go. Except the planning turned out to be the only part of the project that wasn't beset by the most unwelcome and unexpected problems.

I met the cameraman and sound recordist at Heathrow, along with the producer, who I shall diplomatically refer to simply as Mike since he may not relish being reminded of the events surrounding our stay in this most enigmatic of countries. Our roles had been clearly defined: I would direct the visuals, which included establishers of Shakhty, Alexeyev at the gym, chatting with workers at the mine, and organising an afternoon lunch with his family. Mike would focus on the journalistic side, selecting appropriate archive footage and conducting the interview. Olga would meet us at Moscow Airport and take us, courtesy of a hire car and appointed driver, to the Aerostar Hotel, where we could overnight before our schedule started in earnest the following day.

When we arrived in Moscow it took over two hours to work our way through customs, shuffling heel to toe in a freezing, unfriendly concrete Arrivals

Hall, only to have our equipment confiscated, with a demand that we pay additional import duty. In cash, with no receipt. Since everything was legitimately listed on the carnet, a belligerent and seriously annoyed Mike refused to part with any money to 'buy back' our own kit and as soon as we met up with Olga and the driver, he instructed them to take us to the hotel so we could discuss the alternatives with the production office back in London.

The Aerostar was located in Moscow's Belorusskaya neighborhood, not far from the airport, opposite Petrovsky Park. It was breathtakingly opulent, with room service available 24 hours day, recreational amenities that boasted a sauna and fitness facility and spa amenities that included massage rooms and beauty services. It could have been a hotel in any of the major cities of the world, but with one notable difference. The Aerostar, like many of the modern hotels situated near to the airport and in Moscow itself, had been built to show foreign visitors, business executives and potential investors the new face of Russia.

But it did not represent the Russia we were about to discover at the time of our visit; a Russia that had changed to a market-based economy since the dissolution of the Soviet Union; a Russia that had slashed its subsidies to money-losing industries and allowed former state property to be seized by unscrupulous entrepreneurs. Analysts who believed the dismantling of the old administration would raise living standards by allocating resources more efficiently could not have been more off the mark. Since the USSR's collapse, twenty-five per cent of the population lived below the poverty line and life expectancy had fallen. Apart from which, the population was not finding it easy to shake off the old ways of doing things, handed down by countless generations who had been given little choice but to toe the communist line by those who were now embracing their new entrepreneurial opportunities.

Already we had come face to face with a more opportunistic attitude that had left us without our equipment before we had even left the airport, and hasty exchanges were made between Mike and the London office within minutes of our checking in at the hotel reception.

Another unexpected problem came to light when I called by Mike's room to find out what the game plan was. I found him leaning against one of the walls, holding his back, and grimacing. An old sports injury had resurfaced just as he was picking up his baggage. He could hardly walk and the pain was evident. He assured me it would pass after a night's sleep and told me a camera hire company had been contacted in Moscow. In the morning we would set off to find them, hire some replacement equipment, make contact with the Moscow Archive and then take an internal flight to Rostov to meet up with Alexeyev. Since we didn't need to go through customs it was unlikely the authorities would impound the gear since it was being neither imported nor exported.

The next morning Mike didn't appear at breakfast, which was an ominous sign, and when he eventually joined us in the reception area half an hour later with bags duly packed and carried by a porter, he was hobbling slowly and looking even more incapacitated than the night before. He insisted, however, on taking the flight to Rostov, believing his condition would improve. As we crawled our way through the streets of Moscow looking for the equipment hire facility, my nostrils alerted me to the distinct and sickly smell of exhaust fumes. Black smoke poured out of most of the battered vehicles that rattled their way through the city, few of their owners being able to afford to have their cars serviced. We passed several vehicles being pushed because they had broken down, with little hope of an immediate restart. Prostitutes boldly roamed the pavements, plying a trade, we were told, controlled by the police, who issued on-the-spot-fines to the populace for even the least dubious infringement, mostly vehicle related.

The historical fairy-tale domes of St Basil's formed a striking antithesis to these unsavoury present day street scenarios. As we drove past the Moscow River, taking in the unmistakable aroma from the Red October chocolate factory on the far side, we observed people selling ballpoint pens, cleaning products and jewellery from makeshift tables, and I wondered if there really was anyone in Moscow who could supply us with a camera that did not run on clockwork. Eventually we found the hire company and waited while our cameraman and sound recordist made spot checks to test the functionality of the kit, emerging with smiles and a thumbs-up about ten minutes later, effectively clearing us for take-off.

The way the Aeroflot jet buffeted its way through the skies on its one-hour flight to Rostov, barging its way through turbulence, elbowing clouds out of the way and rattling our bones, suggested that Mike might have to be stretchered off as soon as we disembarked so he could have his backbone snapped back into place. It was a terrifying journey, starting at take-off when the cabin crew disappeared behind a red curtain, leaving several semi-drunk passengers to wobble their way down the aisles, knocking back vodka and chain smoking. The only brief acknowledgement they made to the take-offs and landings was to hold onto the rickety seats so they wouldn't fall over.

To distract myself from the horrors of being bumped about in a flying machine tied together by string and prayer mats I gazed out of the window, wondering what other misfortunes could befall us on our journey into the unknown. When I had uprooted my family from London to head east I never intended to travel *this* far east, careering through thin air in a get-me-there-in-one-piece hunk of metal that, God forbid, would be waiting to take us back on a return flight to Moscow just a few days later. Little wonder that Olga and the driver had elected to drive to Rostov.

I shuffled this to the back of my mind and stared down at the forests that were spread out far below, the occasional wooden cabin breaking up the tree lines, thin wisps of smoke spiraling from the chimneys. I wondered how the Russian people had ever managed to communicate during the war years, when vast armies were mobilised through towns, villages and such unyielding terrain, eventually seeing off a German army that had badly miscalculated the harshness of one of the worst Russian winters in recorded history. Daily temperatures fell to 40 degrees below zero and whilst Russian soldiers were well equipped to deal with the extremities of temperature, the Germans had not been issued with warm winter clothing as Hitler believed the invasion would be over before winter. Soldiers froze to death in their sleep, diesel froze in fuel tanks and food was in short supply. The defeat of an entire German army at Stalingrad was considered by many to be the turning point of World War Two, but it was rough justice, paid for heavily in tears and blood.

I remembered from various discussions I'd had with informed researchers on *The World at War* just how much the Russian population had endured. Almost twenty million of them died during the war. In the two-and-a-half-year siege of Leningrad alone there was unparalleled famine caused by the disruption of water, energy and food supplies, resulting in the death of a million and a half soldiers and civilians. Many simply died of starvation in the street, the leather soles from their boots being stripped and used to make soup by those who were surviving on a daily basis. It is incomprehensible that people could live through such a terrible ordeal but Russian history is steeped in unrelenting conflict and catastrophe, stretching as far back as the ninth century.

The landing at Rostov Airport brought me sharply back to the present, as the drunks clung to the backs of the seats, singing and laughing, and I realised that this cocktail of alcohol and optimism was probably the only way they could face the journey on a regular basis.

When we pulled up outside our hotel in Rostov, I thought there must have been some mistake. The building resembled a seaside boarding house that had fallen into disrepair, complete with grimy walls and filthy windows, spread over three floors of creaking floorboards and dodgy banister rails. The hallway smelt of musty carpet soiled by years of vodka and vomit abuse, each floor being occupied by an elderly woman who sat in a chair knitting woolly scarves and hats. I thought these babushkas would retire gracefully by nightfall, but they stayed on guard as self-appointed chaperones of decency, ready to report any unacceptable behaviour to the hotel manager.

Mike, unfortunately, was still in pain and in no better shape and it was clear he would be bedridden for the rest of the trip. Which meant I would now have to undertake the journalistic part of the project as well as directing the pre-arranged sequences. We also discovered that communications were nowhere near as good as they had been at the Aerostar, taking forever to place a call back to London via the hotel switchboard. Added to which our baths had no bathplugs, and the water drizzling from the taps was ice cold and rusty brown. Anticipating that every moment spent in my room I would feel isolated and downright miserable, I decided to take an unscheduled trip to Shakhty with the cameraman to take a look around and meet up with Alexeyev. Olga hastily made the necessary arrangements and during the one hour drive we took the opportunity to go over the following day's filming schedule.

On two occasions we were stopped by roadside patrols who asked to see our documentation. When the second checkpoint patrol began searching through the vehicle, I asked Olga what was going on. She told me some Chechen rebels had kidnapped a group of tourists a couple of days earlier and the police were making spot checks on all vehicles passing through the checkpoints. That didn't sound good. Spending nine months as a hostage in a dank cellar at the behest of a bunch of Chechen rebels wasn't part of the agreement - and it was unlikely that possibility had been listed on the Risk Assessment. With these mounting derailments I was becoming increasingly concerned that I might not make it back to England in time to start the *Stagestruck* project, but Olga assured me the authorities were just taking precautions and, anyway, we weren't tourists, we were journalists.

With apparent immunity from solitary confinement and broken kneecaps we pushed on, arriving at Shakhty late afternoon and immediately embarking on a tour of the town so that I could get a feel for the place. Shakhty (meaning *mine shafts*) is located on the southeastern spur of the Donetsk mountain ridge. In its heyday the town mined some ten million tons of coal a year, until many of the mines were privatised and shut down, causing massive unemployment. Today Shakhty is the main industrial centre of the Eastern Donbass and one of the main producers and exporters of tiles in Eastern Europe. The after effects of Perestroika in 1996 were certainly not in evidence as we watched the townspeople go about their business, shopping, chatting in coffee shops and catching the trolleybuses home. There were trees dotted all over the town and it had a pleasant, homely, atmosphere, far removed from the pollution and excesses of Moscow.

Alexeyev's wife Olimpiada greeted us at the door of their large house and invited us in to meet him. He was a giant of a man, both in height and width, towering over us as if he had just climbed down from his beanstalk to be met by a welcoming party from Lilliput. But whereas his wife had been warm and smiley when she greeted us, Alexeyev seemed cold and unfriendly. We shook hands and followed them through to the living room, where we had a choice of three enormous armchairs to slide into. It was an extraordinary room, spacious and elegant, with a marble fireplace and magnificent Oriental rug. Virtually every shelf and cupboard were adorned with trophies, goblets and bowls, with one wall completely covered in medals.

Since 1970, when Alexeyev had won his first weightlifting medal, he had broken the world record eighty times, the shiny golden medallions twinkling proudly at us proof of his invincibility between 1970 and 1977. Many regarded him as one of the greatest sportsmen of the twentieth century. He was awarded the Order of the Badge of Honour in 1970, Order of the Red Banner of Labour and the Order of Lenin in 1972, and in 1993 he was elected to the International Weightlifting Federation Hall of Fame. And here he was, sitting opposite me, the great man himself in every way.

I told him, through Olga, how we felt honoured to be in his country making a documentary about him, which was obviously a slow process as I had to wait for every question or observation to be translated into

229

Russian and then converted back into English. I realised that the scheduled filmed interview would be a painstaking affair, particularly as he was not currently in the right frame of mind to be put in front of a camera. But it was an integral part of the filming so we needed to warm him up somehow and get him to drop his guard. He seemed suspicious of us, almost as if we were intruding on his time, until Olga told him that we had brought over his fee in American dollars and that we had the first payment with us. Despite the possibility that I was still on the Heathrow blacklist, I had tucked the weighty dollar bills inside my socks at the airport, having been forewarned that carrying cash around in Moscow was not a good idea if you wanted to stay healthy. Mike had the other half of the payment with him, so I handed over my portion to Alexeyev and watched his face crease into a smile. Olimpiada immediately jumped up, announcing that she would make some tea. Alexeyev shook his head almost scornfully, redirecting her to a cupboard, where she removed a large bottle and handed it to him, followed by a handful of glasses, which he distributed around the room.

'Armyanskaya kon'yak,' beamed Alexeyev.

'Armenian cognac,' translated Olga.

'Osobyi.'

'Very special.'

Alexeyev held his glass in the air. 'Khoroshyee zdorove.'

'Good health.'

As the big man downed his glass in one I sensed that to refuse his hospitality on the grounds that the alcohol might startle my internal organs would be to insult him. He was very proud of his cognac and probably had several cases stored in his cellar. 'A gift from an admirer,' Olga informed us. The moment the cognac hit the pit of my stomach I realised that this might be one way we could win his trust. I recalled my first on-screen interview with the businesswoman on *The Business Exchange* and how important it was not to go into an interview situation without first gaining the confidence of the interviewee. So we chatted for a couple of hours about life in Shakhty and he told us how he was the finest cook, gardener, chess player, singer, sports coach and carpenter in the whole of Russia - accomplishments few would be foolish to argue with.

When we left to return to Rostov we had enjoyed two hours of drinking, chatting and laughing, but I was as high as a kite, floating on the ceiling of the car for most of the journey. I had at least had the good sense to push the planned interview back by twenty-four hours just to be sure Alexeyev was definitely on side, and briefed Mike on our visit as soon as we got back to the hotel, including a session discussing some of the intended interview questions to make sure I was in tune with his thinking.

The next morning, having shivered my way through the coldest night I can ever recall, we returned to Shakhty to film Alexeyev talking to old comrades at the mine shaft and giving advice to youngsters at the local gym, where we also met the Mayor of Shakhty, who told us that Vasily Alexeyev was a fine example to the younger people and very much idolised in his home town. We then returned to

231

the house to film some scenes of Alexeyev chopping logs, lifting weighty fence posts and any other activity we could dream up to illustrate a combination of strength and domesticity to use as cutaways over his voice track.

Then we sat down to discuss what we wanted him to talk about during the next day's interview, after which a second bottle of the dreaded Armenian cognac was produced and took centre stage for the next hour or so.

On day three, whilst Olimpiada prepared a lavish lunch to round off our visuals of the great Alexeyev relaxing at home with his family, we filmed the interview using his wall of gold medals as a backdrop. As I feared, the interview began at a plodding pace, but as it progressed, Alexeyev began to open up about his childhood; the forestry work he undertook as a youngster when he had to heave 18 metre logs around all day by hand; his ambition to become an Olympic athlete; his proudest achievements – and his deepest regrets. It was at this juncture that things took an unexpected turn and I realised why he had appeared so sullen and cautious at our first meeting. There were things he wanted to get off his chest; events that had cast a shadow over his enforced retirement and fuelled a bitter distrust of his colleagues, and even his homeland.

His trainers were first in the firing line. His failure to qualify at the Moscow Olympics in 1980 was, according to him, the result of being poisoned by his own coaching staff because they wanted one of their emerging protégés to take over his crown. He told me that during the warm-up, when he was about to walk onto the platform and his weight had reached 150 kilos, he drank from a cup his trainers had given him – a mix of alcohol that would have an effect within a few minutes. Paranoia? An excuse for his failure to win a medal in his own country? We'll probably never know, but it was clear he had been carrying some heavy baggage around that even he had difficulty lifting and discarding.

'What difference does it make? Three times champion, four times champion, the finale in our country is always the same, because nobody needs you. I left all my health in that sport and from sport I have nothing. Because in Russia nobody has any respect for living heroes. Only dead ones. Then they put up monuments, write memoirs, but while you're alive you just get in the way.'

It wasn't what I had been expecting. We were supposed to be filming a celebration of a sporting legend's greatest achievements, not a current affairs special about contest-fixing that most likely could not be substantiated. But I wasn't putting words into Alexeyev's mouth, nor pushing him to furnish us with any details. I asked him if he might have been mistaken; that there might not have been a personal vendetta against him, that he had simply had his time at the top. It served no other purpose than to open up his resentment to another level.

'The writer Volodya Karpov said to me recently: after the Revolution people changed, people became Soviet. Different thoughts. Different goals. And their

inner world changed completely. Take a person after the war. We rebuilt the whole country, and not for pay, nobody got paid then, and nobody sat at home, everybody went out and rebuilt the economy. People aren't like that now. People are spiritually poor. When I was breaking records I was proud of doing something to bring glory to my homeland. Not on the battlefield but on the sports field.

The people of the Soviet Union loved me. They were very proud that the strongest man in the world was a Russian.'

When we concluded the interview I just hoped we had enough material to stay true to the spirit of the series without putting the dampers on it. At the end of the day, though, the man had serious issues. For us to ignore those issues would have been a betrayal of his trust as well as a misrepresentation of the truth.

We spent the next three hours or so filming the lunchtime get-together, cutaways of his medals and cups and personal photographs from his family albums, after which he produced the now obligatory bottle of Armenian cognac. After a couple of glasses I assumed Alexeyev would usher us respectfully to the door and bid us farewell, but the Mayor turned up, all smiles and handshakes, and formally invited us to spend an evening with him at Shakhty's most famous night club. I was amazed that a town like Shakhty even *had* a night club - and more amazed when we took up his offer and found ourselves, less than ten minutes later, in a large, noisy cellar resembling a 1920s speakeasy during Prohibition America, complete with a jazz band, men in tuxedos, women in glitzy dresses and a bevy of scantily-clad waitresses.

It defied belief, but one thing became crystal clear: Alexeyev was wrong about not having respect. The moment he walked in through the door he was greeted with enthusiastic hugs by many of the patrons, all of whom were not just in awe of him but proud that he had adopted Shakhty as his home town. He could hardly claim that his country had left him with nothing when he was surrounded by so much love and affection. There is even a street and a park named after him and a statue was installed in 2014.

Back at the hotel Mike, understandably, had difficulty getting to grips with the interview revelations, although he was probably more disappointed at having to spend another dismal evening lying prostrate on a bed in a cold, grey, bleak room, whilst we were living it up in the warmth and gaiety of Shakhty's celebrated nightspot. Not to mention the fact that he had flown fifteen hundred miles to interview Alexeyev and never even met him.

The next day, he hobbled down from his room and we returned to Moscow along with the nervous and inebriated on our designated Aeroflot flight. I had considered bringing my gifted bottle of Armenian cognac with me to make the trip remotely bearable, but opted instead to give it to one of the babushkas at the hotel for not reporting me to the authorities for repeatedly arriving back at my room in a drunk and disorderly state.

Then we drove around Moscow tidying up loose ends; trying first to find the gym where Alexeyev had trained in the hope that we might track down one of his coaches for an impromptu interview, but without luck; then returning the camera kit to the facilities house, and finally selecting library footage at the Moscow Archives - a frenzied final day that culminated in a safe and relief-fuelled landing at Heathrow at about nine in the evening. It afforded me a moment to remember that when I had returned to London from Los Angeles some years earlier, the city had looked grim and foreboding by comparison, yet on my return from Moscow it seemed the most colourful, vibrant and stimulating place on the planet.

My pre-conceived visions of Russia as a country where the KGB lurked in doorways to interrogate anyone they didn't like the look of and where people vanished for their political affiliations never manifested themselves as a tangible reality, but I did find the country intimidating in many ways, borne, no doubt, of the country's deep-rooted mistrust and intolerance of the west.

There is no denying that Russia and its people have endured a turbulent history and suffered greatly, but perhaps, as with so many countries, it isn't always the enemies amassing at their borders who cause the greatest threat to a nation's well-being as much as the enemy within.

TREADING THE BOARDS

I was looking forward to a period in my life when projects ran smoothly without assailing me with a new set of headaches every day. Russia had been a draining experience but I had little time to pause for breath since *Stagestruck* followed hard on its heels. We were tasked with filming enough material over eleven days to make thirteen twenty-five-minute shows – which meant recording thirty minutes of *usable* content each day. I didn't dwell on the enormity of the task because I was thankful to be back in England safe and sound, secure in the knowledge that the theatre series had been planned with enough precision to afford us a fighting chance of meeting the target dates.

It is only in retrospect that I can reflect on the absurdity of such wishful thinking and realise how close it could have come to disaster. That isn't to say *Stagestruck* was plagued by unforeseen hitches, because it panned out more or less the way I had hoped. It was the fragility of the ground beneath me that I had not taken into serious consideration at the time, or perhaps didn't want to think about; the fact that it could have opened up and dropped us through the cracks at any moment. I had made an agreement with professional venues such as The Theatre Royal, Bury St Edmunds, the sole surviving example of a

Regency playhouse in the UK, to film sequences backstage as well as on the stage area itself, and signed a deal with Anglia TV to use their technicians and edit facilities. This cut down my costs considerably and gave me a certain margin for error, but the post-production schedule was still tight and I could not afford to over-run. And there was another potential problem.

Apart from the handful of contracted theatre professionals I had signed up, every other participant in the shows was an amateur; there were no hard and fast contracts stipulating that they had to attend the filming sessions; just an agreement that we would pay them a performance fee and an opportunity to show off their skills as actors, lighting directors, musicians and set designers to a wider audience than they would normally play to.

I had worked out a format for each show, which was topped and tailed with introductions and end summaries from Christina, with the odd in-vision links, either at an amdram location or on a professional theatre stage. The main body of the shows incorporated workshops, instructional sections, performance and anecdotes and I had attributed rough timings to my running orders. I had already discussed the requirements for the segments with the professional contributors so that on the day they simply covered the agreed ground.

There were two filming methods. The workshops I had little control over because they involved natural interaction between the professionals and the amdram volunteers. The plan was to film them for about twenty minutes, then shoot bridging cutaways so that each item could be edited down later to an acceptable length. With limited edit time back at Anglia, however, the second method had to be more straightforward and involved a professional illustrating how props are made, set designs created, performers stage-managed and so on, talking through the techniques with Christina. I ran one rehearsal prior to filming, and then asked them to make it longer or shorter as appropriate, before committing it to tape. In most instances three takes were enough to knock the section on the head so that we could move on to the next.

Two essential elements ensured *Stagestruck* stayed on course with budget and schedule. Firstly, the amdrams themselves, not one of whom let me down. Every one of them turned up at the required location at the stipulated time, fully prepared for the filming sessions. When you consider there were over two hundred amateur dramatics enthusiasts who eventually appeared on camera throughout the series that was pretty remarkable in itself. I was bowled over by their enthusiasm for the project; few, if any, had aspirations to tread the boards on the West End stage or to be famous, most just relished the diverse range of contributions they could make, whether painting the scenery, operating the lights or supervising the music and sound effects. The amdram circuit didn't just cater for those who liked the idea of 'putting on a show.' Many had joined local groups because they were keen to be involved with the community or wanted to boost their confidence and I was amazed at the lengths some of these societies went to. The Hamlet Theatre Company, for instance, transported lightweight props and scenery to village halls and churches all over the country, erecting makeshift stages complete with lighting rigs and putting on sell-out shows. Sue Heaser of The Wortham Pantomime Group had been creating all her shows from scratch for fifteen years, writing the music and lyrics for original presentations such as *Land of the Flying Moon*, *The Rainbow's End* and *Bumtrinkle's Circus*, all of which have been published and performed worldwide.

Apart from on-screen talent it was imperative to bring on board professional performers and technicians who really knew their stuff and could work at speed without compromise. Christina drew out the very best from all the contributors she appeared with, taking notes from me in between takes and adapting accordingly. Richard Crafter, an experienced lighting cameraman who had worked on countless quality network dramas, lit the scenes for dramatic effect whilst operating hand-held with smooth precision and timing, and Keith Judge edited each show with his usual selective integrity. But for them, and our incredible army of volunteers, the series would not have been received with such enthusiasm by both the viewing public and the commissioners at TLC.

During the making of *Stagestruck* there were no accidents; no catastrophes; no sudden changes of direction or rethinks, no Plan Bs. The pieces of the jigsaw fell into place in a relatively trouble-free, enjoyable and smooth-running five weeks – which was just as well, since the twelve months that followed were destined to become my most frenzied and troublesome ever.

The problems began in March 1997 when we went into pre-production for series two of *The Slow Norris,* our last, as it turned out, with Ultimate Animates. The pre-production phase had passed relatively trouble-free because of the lessons we had learned from making series one, but gave no hint of the underlying discontent that was bubbling under the surface; the result, it seemed, of contractual differences between the puppeteers and HTV. When a promised payment had not been made halfway through filming they felt they had no choice but to down tools until the problem had been resolved. This unfortunate incident held up recording for two hours on a particularly hectic studio day and upset the rhythm of the shoot. Although we had enjoyed a long and rewarding association with these hugely gifted puppeteers, in the end they were unable to reconcile their differences with the company and opted instead to pack their bags and head off to America once we had finished recording.

At around the same time HTV decided to close down its sound stage and convert it into a news complex, a scenario that was to become depressingly familiar with many of the regional ITV stations. I remember on the final day of recording watching a couple of men in hard hats appear on the studio floor taking measurements and marking them down in a notepad. I asked the floor manager if they thought we were filming Bob the Builder and had wandered into the wrong studio but it turned out they were part of the construction team who would be coming in to start knocking the walls down the next day. We asked them to leave. They were interrupting our work and showing no respect for a studio that, over the years, had made many legendary network dramas, from *Return to Treasure Island* to *Robin of Sherwood*; a place where television history had been made but was no longer relevant or wanted. I had the dubious distinction of being the last director to use its legendary studio facilities.

Despite fall-outs with puppeteers and the various takeovers, acquisitions and construction issues that beset production intermittently, the second series of *The Slow Norris* eventually took to the air with over sixty episodes completed, which meant we had managed to side-step the potential mishaps that threatened it from day one.

But my luck was about to run out in the most bizarre of circumstances.

ON ANOTHER PLANET

In his excellent travel book *Notes from a Small Island* Bill Bryson reflects on the wonders of being alive, suggesting that if you were to stop and think about all the things you enjoy most in life you would have few reasons to be truly unhappy – unless, that is, you ever found yourself alone in Weston-Super-Mare on a rainy evening.

As I sat alone in my hotel room at the Grand Atlantic Hotel in Weston-Super-Mare one rainy evening in September 1997, I had cause to reflect on these words, wondering what had possessed me to come back to this dismal seaside resort, with its boy racers and wretched arcade machines and buildings that were a far cry from the town's Victorian heyday. I had not been here since 1975 when I had filmed inserts with Keith Harris and Lenny Henry for their minstrel stage show. Now I was back, working on one of the strangest productions ever.

It had started just as the second series of *The Slow Norris* finished recording and went into post-production. Norris was intended to keep me busy for six months of the year but actually heralded the beginning of five manic years that kept me in the West Country on a semi- permanent basis, despite the fact that I had just moved to the other side of the country.

Dan had been in discussion with King Rollo Films in the UK and Cinar in Montreal about making a thirteen-part co-production based on Jeanne Willis's *Dr Xargle* books, with their ultra-colourful characters and distinctive illustrations by Tony Ross. The stories featured the quirky Dr Xargle, a green alien with five eyes who is a leading expert on life on earth, and his unruly class of Queegles whom he takes on field trips wearing human disguises to teach them about our very strange planet.

Whilst I had been busy wrapping up *The Slow Norris*, the ITV Network Centre had commissioned the series and Andrew Gosling had been contracted as director. Dan invited me to take on the role of producer, which seemed like a good opportunity to gain invaluable experience working alongside one of Canada's leading children's TV producers. The arrangement was that we would develop the scripts with Cinar and King Rollo Films, then film the series in the UK but post-produce in Montreal alongside their team of special effects technicians.

The schedule involved filming drama sequences in and around the Bristol area for the Queegle 'field trips' and a lengthy studio shoot for the scenes inside the classroom on the planet Queeg and aboard the Queegle spaceship. This involved detailed research to find suitable locations and identify a studio to record the classroom scenes now that HTV's facilities were no longer available to us.

There was a period of immense pre-production activity as Andrew, Dan and I met to read through the

244

draft scripts, went out on location recces, scheduled the voice and music recordings and supervised the design of the puppets, including the disguises the Queegles would be wearing on their field trips. Staying true to Tony Ross's book illustrations these would comprise school caps, jackets and tie, socks and shoes. Animated Extras, a prosthetics and animatronics company based at Shepperton Studios took on the task of creating both the puppets and the disguises, working on the costumes first because the location scenes needed to be filmed ahead of the classroom sequences, which required set design and construction as well as more extensive puppet builds and script refinements.

Then we had to audition actors for the various location roles, most importantly the seven parts assigned to the Queegles themselves. Because we needed actors who were small enough to be convincing as the Queegle aliens, our first thought was to use children. The strict guidelines for filming with children, however, combined with the complexities of the shoot, gave us cause to rethink that strategy and we opted instead to hire a group of dwarves.

Once the storylines had been approved, we moved to Bristol for three weeks and set off, with Andy Parkinson as lighting cameraman, filming 'earth' stories that featured the Queegles learning about the weather, food, fashion, gadgets, the seaside, transport, dogs and cats. The old maxim about filming with animals and children was soon to be indelibly changed to never film with animals, children, or anyone running around in surreal prosthetic costumes trying to look normal. Our first location was at a large house where the owners kept numerous cats that lounged about on sofas and in armchairs or fell asleep on bookshelves and in drawers.

The story has long been extinguished from my mind due to the stress of filming roomfuls of Felis domesticus that refused to obey Andrew's instructions and leapt off in every conceivable direction, hissing and baring their claws, the moment he shouted 'Action!' With four of the Queegles chasing after them in bulky, smelly prosthetic costumes with eyeholes that turned out to be too small for accurate geographical orientation, we virtually accumulated an entire series worth of accidents in one horrendous afternoon. Chairs, teacups and vases flew about all over the place as the alien classmates ran riot in cat hell. After some quick on-the-spot thinking we broke down the cat segments into more manageable bite-sized chunks, rounding up and isolating just a few cats at a time in order to make the task more controllable.

We didn't fare much better on day two at our fictional dog show. The dog handlers were used to enticing their animals to perform with actors but weren't altogether sure how to persuade them to interact with a troupe of dwarves running around in freakish disguises. It was difficult to know who were the most alarmed, the owners, the dogs or the Queegles, but the canines viewed the Queegles as chase fodder, running them to ground at every opportunity and chewing frantically at their costumes. We spent more time rescuing the dwarves from the clutches of these over-excited dogs than we did filming. On one occasion, Rebel Queegle – played by a usually patient chap called Brian – ran recklessly towards Andy Parkinson who had positioned his camera at ground level. Brian, in a blind panic and with a snarling dog at his heels, had no idea he was on a collision course with the camera, and our shouts of *'Stop!'* had little effect since Brian could neither see nor hear particularly well surrounded as he was by a wall of foam, and carried on running until he collided with Andy and literally bounced over the top of him, landing on his back in a breathless heap. All that was missing was the *BOOIING!* sound. As I looked down at Brian sprawled on the ground in front of me, listening to dogs running around in circles barking, Queegles shouting, and general chaos going on all around, I feared that Brian might be badly injured, or dead, so we hauled him up and hastily unzipped his costume. Thankfully the padding had given him maximum protection on impact so he was just winded, though not in the least bit amused. The other Queegles came bounding over as Brian recovered, clearly angry about the situation and fed up with the limited control they had inside the confines of the costumes. Day Two and already I had a mutiny on my hands, although to be fair, they did have a point.

I always thought the buck stopped with the director but apparently when the producer is on location, it's his call, which in this instance was me. So I told them how sorry I was that things hadn't quite gone to plan and assured them there were no more scenes involving animals, and tomorrow we would be on the beach building sandcastles and having fun in the amusement arcade on the pier. I'm not sure they were wholly convinced but agreed to carry on without any adjustments being made to the costumes, which frankly would have kept the wardrobe department up half the night and may not have looked too good on camera.

That evening, having checked in at the Grand Atlantic, I went over the schedule with Andrew and John Parris to see if we could simplify the following day's action, but concluded that it would involve drastic script changes that might diffuse the humour and it would be better to stick to Plan A. When we went down for supper we discovered that the restaurant and ballroom had been taken over by a wedding reception, so Andy Parkinson and I decided to cut loose and visit a Greek restaurant we had seen in the town earlier. It made for a pleasant evening, away from the pressures of a situation that was as alien to us as it was to Xargle himself and we reminisced about our time on the road with Venom and the other Black Metal bands that now seemed sane and well-ordered by comparison.

We returned to the Grand Atlantic at about eleven o'clock to find that the dwarves had now infiltrated the wedding reception and were dancing with the bride, the bridesmaids and several of the guests. I considered hauling them out but thought what the hell, they'd had a couple of shitty days, the bride and groom seemed to be enjoying their company and, anyway, wasn't it turning out to be that kind of a shoot?

The next day we assembled on the beach and filmed numerous seaside-type sequences that didn't involve seawater, dog saliva, or other substances likely to dissolve or damage the costumes. Or attract too much attention. Some hope. The intended scenarios, which included sand-castle building competitions and beach games with some of the local children, fell apart fairly quickly when the children, intimidated by the appearance of a bunch of strange alien creatures, abandoned their buckets and spades and went scurrying in panic back to their parents. Andrew did manage to persuade the actors to participate in a spot of donkey riding, despite my assurances to them that animals wouldn't be on the agenda, sold possibly on the fact that they were old, arthritic and heavily blinkered.

As I stood well out of the way on the promenade watching Queegle Mayhem, I heard a voice next to me say: 'What the hell is going on?'

It was a reporter from one of the local newspapers who happened to have been passing and was completely bemused by the sight of his normal Weston-Super-Mare summer beach idyll being turned into a crazed Cartoon Land. I stared out nonchalantly at the chaotic scene.

'They were doing okay until the LSD kicked in.'

He looked at me suspiciously, not sure if I was being serious or not. There was certainly no denying that none of the people in our line of vision were behaving rationally. When he started scribbling notes, I decided I'd better set him straight before his readers got the wrong end of the stick.

'We're filming a TV show. For children. No drugs, just unlimited chaos.'

249

'Ah. Right.' He nodded. Children had an empathy with the weird and the surreal even if adults were rendered mystified and bewildered by things they couldn't explain. Always happy to provide the local rag with publicity, I gave him as much background information as possible and watched as he scanned his notes wondering how his editor would fit in a story about an extra-terrestrial beach invasion alongside articles about unwanted high-rise developments, traffic warden strikes, and the opening of a new outdoor swimming pool by the mayor.

I left him to ponder the problem whilst we decamped and headed off to the pier to record the Queegles exploring the wonders of the entertainment arcade. Overnight rain had made the decking area quite dangerous and as the Queegles began slipping and sliding all over the place there were a couple of heart-stopping moments when I thought they might actually skid under the barriers, or bounce over the top of them, into the sea. Whilst the costumes would doubtless give added buoyancy in such circumstances it occurred to me that I had not foreseen a situation where the Queegles might be floating about in the Bristol Channel, and wondered if I should have asked Animated Extras to fit distress flares and whistles as an added precaution.

With the help of the production team we were able to manoeuvre them into the arcade area and position them on the various rides, including the helter-skelter and dodgems, and even managed to film a sequence inside the Haunted House where in low light they looked even scarier than the house residents. Three of the Queegles then attempted to run across a castle rampart comprised of rolling metal tubes but lost their balance, and after three or four seconds of ungainly leg whirring, collapsed and found themselves dumped in an ungainly heap at the castle gates. After that we went on Red Alert, poised to jump in and rescue any Queegle who looked like he might be at risk from being tossed from the rickety platforms or sucked into the machinery, and after two hours we emerged back into daylight and the bracing sea air, with all limbs intact and unbelievably nobody the worse for wear.

Two more days of filming followed that I'd rather not dwell on, until finally we returned to the sanctuary of our London office to start organising the main studio shoot. Whilst we had been having a simply wonderful time by the seaside, Deborah O'Boyle the designer had been hard at work constructing the studio sets for Queegle Planet and the sections were being delivered and installed at the studio in Hayes.

Before shooting could commence, however, we needed to record the voice tracks with an assortment of voice artists, headed by the satirist, cartoonist and performer Willy Rushton, who played Dr Xargle. Then we wheeled them into a second sound studio to record the songs that had been written by the prolific John Du Prez.

When we finally gathered for the studio shoot the schedule was recklessly tight, based on an agreed co-production agreement with Cinar that Andrew and I would take the first six completed shows to Montreal so that their technicians could create the special effects (the Queegle spaceship hurtling through space and so on) and we could mix the sound tracks. With so many Queegle characters in the shows the studio now resembled an over-subscribed puppeteer's convention. Add to this extensive roll-call our technical crew and production personnel, Deborah's chippies working with saws and hammers on a few yet-to-be-completed set sections and props, and the sound playback of Queegle bedlam in words and song, I found myself entering an abstract subterranean world that became, rather unnervingly and frighteningly, an accepted part of my normal working day.

Andrew and John Parris did a sterling job keeping everything on track, helped by the puppeteers' commitment and a turnaround system that enabled them to rest their arms between the demanding set-pieces so nobody dropped from exhaustion, and by late November the first six shows had been filmed, edited, and made ready for their final tweaking in Canada.

Andrew and I were excited at the prospect of spending ten days in Montreal but it took a while to acclimatise to everyday working life in a city where the temperatures dipped to minus thirty in the evenings and froze our ears and noses before we had even managed to walk a hundred yards in the snow. At one point one of Andrew's shoes had come off en route to Cinar's office and he hadn't even noticed because his feet were so numb. We did warm to the city itself though because it was so diverse. Cinar's producers and technical teams were welcoming and accommodating and their facilities impressive, and it was rewarding to see the visual effects come together so effectively. In between successful days spent finalising the shows, we explored as much of Montreal as we could, with its bustling streets, shops and modern sculptures; beautiful historic buildings like the Notre-Dame basilica; the Olympic park, built in 1976 but now abandoned; the Old Port, where the rusting railway lines stood as testament to the old traditional methods of import and export, the frozen dock area providing a natural ice rink for skaters who span and twirled to the music of Elton John, and the restaurants where everybody spoke English but infuriatingly only spoke French the moment you sat down to order a meal.

I made one final visit the following March to finalise the remaining shows, without Andrew this time because he was engaged on another project. Montreal in the spring was something of a revelation, the ski jackets, gloves and hats having been replaced by T-shirts, shorts and flip-flops, everyone's smiles reflecting their relief at the welcome change of season. It was odd to be in a major city on my own, with no one to share the experience, so I was pleased when the last of the shows was completed and I was able to return to the UK ready to dispatch the transmission copies to the Network Centre.

All we had to do now was sit back and wait for the critical acclaim that our endeavours would surely be worthy of; enjoying the moment when *Dr Xargle* flew to the top of the ITV ratings tree, virtually guaranteeing a second series.

Except the shows were not re-commissioned, which was a huge disappointment for everyone involved in the production. Admittedly the series was more surreal than anything children's television had been broadcasting at that time and probably came as something of a culture shock to executives and audience alike, but some constructive criticism would have been useful, even if it meant we had to make substantial changes for a second series.

In retrospect I can only think that younger children found it confusing and older children just didn't get it. More fundamentally there may have been a likely lack of credibility, the zany Queegle Planet characters having little visual correlation with the class that embarked on the field trips in human disguises.

There is no question that Jeanne's *Dr Xargle* stories are mini masterpieces and Tony Ross's illustrations works of art, the books today being as popular as ever, with larger-than-life characters that fly off the pages. But whilst we had done our utmost to replicate both the spirit and the innovation of the Queegles, hindsight tells me that the series would probably have worked better as animation because it needed to maintain its fantasy element without brushing so dramatically with reality. Because the planet aliens in the spaceship looked different from the prosthetic-clad class out on the locations, we probably should have considered adapting the stories at script meetings so that each episode contained a dramatic turning point where the aliens risked being discovered because of an action that would reveal their true identity, their yellow fur spilling out, clearly visible, from their uniforms at frequent intervals.

But all this happened over twenty years ago. Whether the series would be received any differently now we will never know, but I had little time to reflect on where modifications could have been made, because another series of *The Slow Norris* had been commissioned and was about to take my focus again. For the next three years, in fact, the Norris production unit became a team of wandering nomads because there were no longer any suitable sound stages available to us in the Bristol area. The sets that had been put into storage locally ended up being transported to Meridian Studios in Southampton for two seasons and Maidstone Studios in Kent for the fifth and final series. In the wake of Ultimate Animates' departure, Phil Eason had joined us as co-ordinating puppeteer, with Todd Jones taking on the demanding role of Slow Norris, and Mak Wilson operating Ally. Because the working practice was well established the shows were made with the least amount of fuss and bother and it's a series I am still particularly proud of.

By the end of its five-year run I thought that the world of puppetry and visual misdirection could no longer offer any further challenges or unforeseen surprises. I should have known better.

BACK TO THE TOYSHOP

As we know, when one trap-door closes another one opens.

Although I had spent the best part of a decade working on puppets shows, I had not had any serious exposure to the more intricate world of animatronics, apart from the simple electronic eye-and-mouth operations required to animate The Slow Norris and a couple of the characters on Planet Queegle.

All that was about to change.

Dog and Duck was another idea Dan had been developing to take over from *The Slow Norris* when the giant sloth and Ally had exhausted all of their story possibilities and something equally stimulating and challenging was needed to replace them. *Dog and Duck* certainly met those requirements. Apart from a couple of traditional hand puppets, most of the characters in the new show were to be complex animatronics, including a dog that could wag its tail, rolls its eyes and wiggle its nose as it moved around on four wheels, and a duck that could not only glide around the set on two wheels but also flap her wings.

The proposal that had won the commission arrived on my doorstep in the spring of 1999 and at first it sounded intriguing and delightfully uncomplicated:

Joe and Jenny, two children, have moved with their parents to an old, tumbledown house in the country. They have brought with them their two inseparable toy companions - Joe's rather scruffy old dog on wheels and Jenny's duck. But whenever they go off to school, or go out for the day, or go to sleep, Dog and Duck come alive and set off to discover the real world this new house contains.

So far so good. An excellent premise for a child's fantasy adventure. Sounded like fun. I read on excitedly:

As Dog and Duck explore, they unlock mysteries. The house is alive with a life of its own. Some things we can see straight away - why didn't we realise that the old piano in the corner of the hall could play and sing by itself; why did we imagine that the old cardboard puppet theatre in the attic had no ability to tell us a story by itself; why did we ever think you could only sit and watch the television in the kitchen and not ask it to show you answers to your questions?

And why did I think Dan would never dream of asking me to take on a series that was a hundred times more complicated than anything we had done before, based on a standard ITV budget that could never compete with a drama or cinema feature? With unseen worlds, a piano whose keys played themselves, a puppet theatre and a television that came to life to tell their own stories.

Whilst my first thought should have been to take Dan's imaginative scenario into my arms and embrace it with undiluted enthusiasm, it was what was *not* written into the proposal that occupied my immediate thoughts. Like, what would happen to our recording days if any of the animatronics went down, or the piano wires snapped? How exactly was the puppet theatre going to magically spring into life? How would we schedule the complexities of animatronics with the limited 'on set' time we would have filming with real actors and children? These and other questions formed the basis of a lengthy list I drew up for discussion when I met with Dan and Tracey Mulcrone, the producer, a few days later. They had also been giving serious thought to the potential problems.

Animated Extras would build both the animatronics and the props and be in attendance 24/7 during the recordings, with a back-up team engaged exclusively to fix any mechanical breakdowns. There would be two Dogs and two Ducks so that one, or both, could be replaced at any time in case of technical failure (with Dog alone costing reputedly the same as a Ferrari, that was one hell of an investment). The puppet theatre would involve animated inserts and no live shooting, and the TV set and the children's toy box would be manned by hand puppets. Which just left us with the problem of finding a studio, since HTV no longer had one.

The answer to that not insignificant conundrum would become one of our biggest headaches. It was decided that *Dog and Duck* would use a real house instead of a studio; a natural location with real rooms and a real garden, with surrounding trees and vistas. Which sounded fine on paper but did not account for the biggest enemy a director and a Director of

258

Photography can encounter on a shoot: variable lighting conditions. Not to mention a need for adequate operating space. Or somewhere to situate the control gallery with the necessary extensive cable links between the walls and the floors. Or the ability to move heavy equipment through narrow doorways and up and down flights of stairs on a regular basis.

Since the interiors would be filmed in traditional drama style there could be days when master shots might be recorded with sunshine spilling into the rooms and their corresponding reverse shots recorded some hours - or days - later when it might be overcast and pouring with rain. A standard bedroom is relatively small and not ideal for accommodating two mobile animatronics characters, three camera operators, three cameras and cables, lights and lighting stands, a floor manager, a hand puppet and two animatronics operators. Keeping track of prop continuity and the positioning of characters for the reverse shots would also need some careful thought, since constantly spinning back to videotape points to check them would be time-consuming and risk damage to the tapes themselves.

Most of the difficulties were solved without too much head-banging, although the lighting problem was destined to hinder us on a regular basis. The puppeteers, headed by Phil Eason, would operate the animatronics from a separate bedroom, viewing the scenes on their own monitors, with wide angle lenses being used on all the cameras to make the rooms appear much larger than they actually were. The trick now would be to co-ordinate all of the departments so that everyone was up to speed on how the technical aspects of the shoot would be achieved, most notably the design unit, headed by Mike Joyce, who elected to use the traditional Polaroid method of taking instant photographs to keep track of continuity.

We eventually found a detached house that suited our requirements in Blagdon, on the outskirts of Bristol, which had three floors, with reasonable sized rooms and a good expanse of garden. Thankfully the living room and dining area had been converted into one enormous room on the ground floor, which meant we could sub-divide the area into a hallway and a kitchen, with false, moveable walls that gave us the space and flexibility we needed to film without restriction. It also meant we could slide various props such as the sink and washing machine out of the way whenever we needed to reposition the cameras or the lights.

It was a complex jigsaw puzzle we actually enjoyed getting to grips with, made all the more satisfying when our first recording day approached and we knew that most of the seemingly insurmountable problems had been resolved, aided by the usual sprinkling of anxiety and adrenaline that keeps any production unit on its toes.

There were, of course, some unknowns that we still had to consider. There was a high percentage of filming required in the garden area, for instance, which meant it was imperative to schedule in weather cover. Drenching the cameras, cables and animatronics in rain would not have done them any favours and most likely delayed the shoot indefinitely, so various Plan Bs were put in place, ready to be brought into play if we had to hurriedly reschedule or we ran out of filming time with the children.

A team of writers was contracted to draft the sixty-five scripts and once again the task of tailoring their imaginations to the filming practicalities had to be addressed. With animation you can embark on the wildest of fantasies - with puppets and animatronics you cannot. Dog was quite large and heavy for operating in a confined space. For him to turn around - a straightforward action for a puppet, an animated character, or a human - involved a complex three-stage radio-controlled manoeuvre that would not only look cumbersome on camera but risked inviting technical mishaps. Neither Dog nor Duck could jump down from cupboards or climb stairs so we had to create the illusion that they could, employing time-dissolves or inserting bridging shots between the edit points. I knew that a script section which had Dog sitting on a window ledge talking to Duck, then joining her halfway through his dialogue, would be devoid of any seamless visual flow unless we could apply a practical solution to that transition. The mechanics of filming the series were littered with these kinds of challenges, but since we did not want to burden the writers with too many do's and don'ts, we opted to review the completed scripts before they were converted into shooting scripts and find ways of choreographing the action.

After I had marked up my floor plans we were ready to take on the task of making it all work within the specified time frame, starting with the recording of the voice tracks and music, featuring Josie Lawrence as Duck, James Fleet as Dog and Gary

Martin as Piano. James was well known for his appearances in *Four Weddings and a Funeral* and *The Vicar of Dibley*, and Josie was an established comedienne and actress best known for her work with the Comedy Store Players improvisational troupe and the television series *Whose Line Is It Anyway?* Working with this team was a pure joy, the interaction between them so precise, their interpretation of the scripts delivered with such vitality and professionalism, that it generated some much needed confidence among the creative team as we geared up for the production phase.

And so, in the summer of 1999, a unit of thirty-eight production personnel, including actors Alison Sterling and John McAndrew and youngsters Carrie Fletcher (Jenny) and Jack Snell (Joe) assembled at the house in Blagdon, ready to transform it into Dog and Duck's secret world of fun and magic. For the majority of the time it *was* fun. We had pre-recorded the visual effects of Dog 'disappearing' through various walls in the house, the remaining special effects being achieved with simple chromakey backgrounds, whilst composer John Du Prez had, with his usual ingenuity, wired a computer containing his music tracks to the piano prop, so that its keys were invisibly pressed down in time with the music, and Piano's lips moved in synch with the dialogue playback. The only minor drawback was that the soundtrack needed to be played back at an inordinately high level for the puppeteers and animatronics operators to hear it and respond with mouth and head movements. Knowing that our immediate neighbours might be driven to despair by the sounds of puppet characters talking and singing all day long for weeks on end, we came to an amicable arrangement with them that involved appropriate financial remuneration for the inconvenience.

Everyone was happy. A little daunted by what lay before them, perhaps, but happy nevertheless. I can only recall two instances from the first series, in fact, when filming was threatened with any long-term stoppages. The first involved a mechanical breakdown of Dog, who had spent most of the morning veering out of control and crashing into walls, and Piano, whose wires had snapped, rendering its keys inoperable. They both required extensive repairs and since our back-up Dog had become victim to mechanical failure the day before we were left with Duck as our only working animatronic. Finding a suitable scene that involved Duck acting on her own proved more difficult than we had envisaged. There were several scenes we could shoot in the kitchen area but the design unit had spent four hours dressing the set for a surrealist dream sequence involving fifty teacups suspended on invisible wires, a bubble machine and thirty-eight toy penguins. Analysing the time it would take to make a design switch or wait for repairs to the animatronics, we went for the only remaining option, which was to transfer the entire technical unit up two floors to the attic, where Duck could interact with the puppet theatre. It took two hours to make the move and pushed the schedule back accordingly.

A couple of weeks later we were filming a scene on the patio involving eight-year-old Jack (Joe) and

Mum, who was teaching him to ride his new bicycle. Although Mike Joyce had produced a shiny new bike, complete with an impressive range of gears and flashing lights, it was pink and Jack was not at all happy about that. I apologised and told him that it was the best we could do. He declined to ride it on the basis that it was a girl's bike (which it was). I reminded him that I was the director and if I wanted him to ride the pink bike then that was the way it would have to be. He stared defiantly at me, folded his arms and refused point blank to ride it.

Sensing that my negotiation skills were taking a turn for the worse and with the entire production crew standing by keenly awaiting the outcome, I told him I would probably feel the same in his position and would therefore turn the bike another colour in post-production. Was there any particular colour he preferred? We settled on light blue, sealed the deal with a hi-five, he rode the bike, and thanks to the god of technology we managed to turn it blue in the edit suite a few weeks later. It was a narrow squeak, though, and I stayed on constant alert for any further situations that might incur child actor mutiny destined to scupper my plans.

ANIMAL MAGIC

As summer surrendered its smiley face to autumn, and autumn was replaced by a bitterly cold winter, we concluded filming of the first series of *Dog and Duck* and the unit disbanded to take a well-earned break while the house was left to see out the Christmas period in eerie desolation, devoid of the music and laughter it had enjoyed throughout the summer months. I suspect the neighbours were mighty pleased to see the back of us and must have relished having their peace and tranquillity back.

Because the series had been edited on site at the house location in tandem with the shoot, we were ready to take the completed shows into the sound dubbing theatre a few days after the final scenes had been filmed and the rough-cuts approved. We had reached an agreement with Anglia Television for me to mix the sound tracks in Norwich, which meant I could spend the next two months putting the series to bed on home turf.

Nigel Pickard at the Network Centre was delighted with the results and in the New Year commissioned *Dog and Duck* for a second series, as we had hoped. A huge investment had been made initially in building the animatronics, the composition of dozens of songs, background music and links, animation, titles and set design and with these set-up costs out of the way it was a good opportunity to utilise the new budget to ease pressure on the production. By good fortune it also meant we could continue renting the Blagdon house and maintain continuity of location, despite all the problems the building had given us.

But it wasn't all good news. Nigel wanted a staggering one hundred and twenty shows for the second series. Yikes. Dreaming up that many new ideas was going to take a massive amount of brain mangling before we could even give consideration to the pre-production phase. For one director to handle that many shows was an immense ask, so I assumed Dan and Tracey would bring on board a second director to share the workload. They were several steps ahead of me and had already divided the shows up between four directors who would take on thirty shows each, scheduled across the four seasons, my segment being designated for the summer. A brainstorming session was hurriedly organised with Dan, Tracey, script editor Jo Killingley and the writing team at a country hotel near Bristol, where it was agreed I would write twelve scripts for the new shows, a necessary stop-gap now that a potential six month's work had been whittled down to three and I had not lined up any work for the spring.

By a quirk of fate I discovered that the BBC was looking for a Producer/Director to work on *The Animal Magic Show,* a series combining puppetry with magic and based, with due irony, in Bristol, on a six month contract, starting early spring and continuing right through the summer months into the autumn. It was, of course, too good to be true, but by

266

now I was in my early fifties, which would seem positively ancient to all the eager bright young things who frequented the children's department of the BBC.

But ill winds were beginning to blow through ITV, with more personnel and department cuts being made, including children's production, so I needed to seriously consider the alternatives. I posted off my application and was delighted, if somewhat surprised, to be called for an interview with Nigel Pope, the executive producer, accompanied by the BBC's head of HR. I travelled back down to Bristol full of apprehension but the meeting went better than expected. Nigel was very responsive, seemed impressed by my track record, including my interest in magic that had prompted me to draft my thirty-page proposal for a series on the history of magic, *Smoke and Mirrors,* some years earlier.

Two days later HR called me back to offer me the job. Unbelievable. I had not worked for the BBC for thirty-four years, and never as a director. I would also be jumping ship a second time, but my survival instincts were kicking in and it was important I expanded my choices – particularly if there was now a possibility of ongoing work with the BBC.

Dan was initially disappointed that I would not be available to take on the summer segment of *Dog and Duck* but happy for me to take on the winter session as soon as *The Animal Magic Show* was finished. I agreed, even though I knew the winter filming period at the Blagdon house would potentially be the most difficult, with less daylight hours, freezing temperatures, the area around the house potentially awash with rainwater, mud and ice, and working with a production crew who would be weary after an intense and demanding nine months at the location.

I pushed all that to the back of my mind. Winter was a lifetime away and I needed to refocus. In early April I rented an apartment near to the BBC studios in Whiteladies Road and took up my role as Producer/Director on *The Animal Magic Show*. The programme had already enjoyed a first series which Nigel himself had produced and directed, but with other commitments on upcoming wildlife shows, he was happy to hand over the reins and keep a watchful eye as Executive Producer. The task now was for me to make the next thirteen shows as good as the first thirteen, if not better.

The first thing I noticed when I took up residence at the BBC Bristol studios was how relaxed everyone was. No constant looks of panic on people's faces; no running down corridors as if a fire or civil war had just broken out; no Assistant Directors scurrying around with walkie-talkies blurting out urgent, distorted messages from their belt clips. There was a disarming serenity to the place, as if nothing could faze anyone; so laid back it was positively pastoral. During my first week I remember taking a call from a producer at the BBC studios in Glasgow who was making a radio show about hidden camera filming. He had somehow discovered my involvement with the *Candid Camera* series and was keen to interview me, live on air, that evening, at ten minutes past six. I told him I was busy organising a show in Bristol and there was no way I could make it to Glasgow in time. No problem. He would arrange a link-up between the

Bristol and Glasgow studios so I merely had to take five minutes out of my schedule for a brief, impromptu, on-air chat. Always happy to give publicity to *Candid Camera* I agreed, but when I turned up at the sound studio at six o'clock that night, I discovered it was locked and in complete darkness. I looked around, wondering if I had gone to the wrong studio. I enquired at the main reception desk, slightly panic struck. The receptionist made a couple of quick internal calls and established that I was, indeed, in the right place and someone would be down shortly to open up.

At five minutes past six, a middle-aged lady wearing over-sized glasses and a world-weary expression appeared in the corridor jangling a set of keys and ambling along as if time was a meaningless entity within her private universe. She nodded at me with casual aplomb, then turned her attention to the locked door, trying each key in rotation without success. I hovered anxiously over her shoulder as she moved her eyes closer to the lock, squinting as she inspected each jagged metal stick and jiggled it with mild annoyance.

Eventually the door swung open and the lights were turned on. The clock on the studio wall told me it was nine minutes past. Jesus! Now what? Then I heard a distorted voice calling out to me from a pair of headphones lying on the desk. 'Bob. Are you there, Bob?'

I raced over to the desk, put on the headphones, pulled out my notes, and sat down. 'I'm here. Had a problem…'

'Okay. Stand by. You're on air in twenty seconds.'

I heard music being faded up in my ears, followed by a second voice saying 'and now we journey back to the nineteen-seventies, when ace prankster Jonathan Routh played tricks on unsuspecting members of the public courtesy of the iconic *Candid Camera* series. Bob Harvey, the editor on that series, is here with us now. Bob, tell us your most vivid memories of your time on *Candid Camera*.'

I glanced at my notes then launched into a manic jumble of recollections, unaware of how much time I actually had to rattle it all off. I hardly paused for breath until the voice cut back in and said, 'that was fascinating, Bob, thanks very much for your insight into such a wonderful series.' I said something like it was a pleasure, but as the sound in my headphones faded away I realised I had no further contribution to make and had been discarded, with the click of a switch, in favour of the next item.

'Thanks, Bob,' said the first voice. 'I'll send you a cassette copy.'

And that was it. I peeled off the headphones and sat in the small room, wondering what had just happened. One minute I was imparting pearls of wisdom, live, to the nation, and the next I was sitting on my own in deadly silence. My moment of fame had lasted nowhere near the fifteen minutes Andy Warhol had promised me and I had been dumped back into a world where time seemed completely meaningless again.

I left the lady with the over-sized glasses to turn off the lights and lock up and wandered back to my office, wondering how many of BBC's radio transmissions were conducted with the same casual application. My new environment was obviously one that would take some getting used to.

The Animal Magic Show production team comprised just three people: Me, Vanessa Coates, the production secretary, and Rob Yeoman, a film researcher who seemed to know his way around the film archives as if he had been born on one of the shelves that housed the hundreds of rows of film cans. An initial thirteen themed programme ideas had already been drawn up and two writers, Robin Kingsland and Paul Brophy, had submitted first draft scripts. They were informative and filled with hilarious one-liners, many relating to animals, others relevant to the subject matter, be it fashion, art, flowers or country customs. Anthony Owen, our magic consultant, had adapted a variety of tricks to fit in with these themes, so my first job was to co-ordinate all of this thinking, assimilate the practical realities, and convert the drafts into final, workable studio scripts.

My initial script reading with Dominic Wood, the magician and entertainer who was fronting the shows, and Brian Herring, the puppeteer operating Billy Nibbles, proved to be an education in itself. They had worked together on the first series and established an impressive working relationship. All I had to do was wind them up, let them go and watch as they went through their lines, improvising and developing the material with sharply observed wit and innovation. From that first reading I knew that as long as I gave them the space to make creative contributions,

271

everything would turn out fine. When we met for subsequent readings, I took along my pocket memo recorder and taped everything Dom and Brian said so that I could play it back later while I was refining the scripts. It was far easier than the three of us frantically scribbling amendments to the drafts before they slipped through our collective memory bank.

Working with those two was a sheer delight. I had not laughed so much in ages and it set the scene for one of the most enjoyable periods of my career; endless weeks when nothing was urgent and the days passed with a remarkable but welcome absence of stress and anxiety.

A few weeks before we were due to move into the studio to start recording, I organised a trip to the prop-builders in Manchester to check that all the big illusions were working properly and wouldn't let us down on the day. Dom and Anthony went through their specified routines and discovered numerous adjustments that needed to be made to the props. Being able to discuss modifications with the designers in Manchester saved us a lot of wasted studio time standing around watching people with saws, hammers and welding torches make the necessary refinements. Which meant that by the time everything was shipped to the studio at the end of July we were able to hit the ground running.

For reasons I cannot remember the BBC had decided to hire the studios at Teddington Lock. I hadn't been back there since I had directed *Comic Cuts* nine years previously. Nothing much had changed, except that Thames Television no longer held its broadcasting franchise and was now hiring out its facilities to anyone looking for studio space at a reasonable price. The old *World at War* production block had been knocked down (thankfully not burned down) and replaced with a scenery storage area, and the place was devoid of the buzz of activity I had become accustomed to. No longer did the directors and stars of the country's top-rated dramas and situation comedies roam the corridors, spilling into the bar and restaurant, regaling each other with amusing anecdotes and reminiscences. Now it was frequented by a new generation of programme makers who walked in their ghostly slipstream, drifting around with furrowed brows, troubled, possibly, by having to produce programmes that would hopefully attract a high audience rating on limited studio time, with vastly reduced budgets.

On *The Animal Magic Show* we had no such worries. Not only had I been given ample time to organise the shoot, we were only recording one show a day – a luxury to someone used to battling to record five or six complex shows back-to-back within the same time frame. I had elected not to over-complicate the shoot with unwieldy and costly sets but had settled for a simple white backdrop onto which we could project gobo images relevant to the stories: birds in flight, flowers, dinosaurs, and so on. Guy Littlemore, the camera supervisor, then adjusted the background colours accordingly, orange for a hot desert in the Safari show, light blue for Water, dark blue with twinkling white dots for night-time scenarios. We even found some old props lying around in the storage area, including a mangy camel once used on *The Benny Hill Show,* which we gave a new lease of life for our desert backdrop. Since the background could never have competed with the charisma of our two star performers, Dominic Wood and Billy Nibbles, visual energy was achieved with the minimum of set dressing. Which meant we could devote our time to the execution of the illusions and developing every aspect of the on-screen magic, not least of which was the way Brian Herring brought his glove puppet alarmingly to life. One minute Billy was a limp piece of material lying across the prop top hat in the middle of the set, the next he was transformed into a cheeky, vibrant, scheming furry animal, full of invention and wicked facial expressions - and incredibly funny. His energetic capers were matched by Dom's unrelenting enthusiasm for the shows, and there wasn't anything he wouldn't try in order to keep it fresh and entertaining, including wearing a skimpy caveman leopard skin for the Dinosaur themed show, being bashed over the head by a giant club, and having a bucket-load of baked beans poured over him during the Disappearing Baked Beans trick.

Then, in the blink of an eye, one of the most enjoyable periods of my career was over and we vacated the studio. The next week I returned to Bristol and set about editing and sound mixing the shows, then delivered them to Nigel Pope. And that was that. No ongoing contract or suggestion there might even be one. Another series put to bed and time to move on to the next.

At the end of October I returned to the house at Blagdon ready to film the remaining thirty *Dog and Duck* shows, but it was an unsettling experience.

Apart from the camera crew and puppeteers, most of the production personnel were new and the location itself looked bleak and uninviting, not helped by continual downpours and cold winds that whipped around the building on an almost daily basis. It was also pitch black when we turned up at eight each morning to start work. We had to trudge from the designated car park area, now covered in mud, to the house, using torches to find our way. More significantly, we lost daylight at about half-past three, which meant that if we hadn't completed any exterior scenes by then, or the weather turned from bad to impossible, we either had to erect canopies, create our own daylight, or re-schedule completion for another day. Which would give Mike Joyce and his team more continuity headaches. The design unit had already encountered practical difficulties filming some of the autumn exteriors. Because the garden area had been landscaped initially on top of clay and the rainwater was not draining away quickly enough, large wooden boards had to be placed across the flooded areas, supporting lights, cables and cameras in a curious and precarious configuration.

We diligently worked our way through those difficult and daunting weeks, frustrated occasionally by the kind of animatronics failures that moisture and ice invariably cause, with Plan Bs ready to be put into play whenever we ran out of filming time with the children or couldn't match the light, or both. There were various British soap operas and dramas that were being filmed entirely on location at that time, most notably *The Bill, Brookside,* and *Eldorado*. But these shows employed actors and not animatronics, none of whom had to say their lines to playback, or break into song, and the directors didn't have the problem of creating a cornucopia of visual effects. Whilst these soaps might have occasionally been accused of manufacturing storylines that were off-the-wall, their characters were not required to actually walk through them in the same way ours were. And unlike *Eldorado* we weren't blessed with long days of endless warmth and sunshine.

The sun certainly wasn't a regular visitor to Blagdon in November and early December and the Chew Valley was constantly flooded. One evening I left the premises late at night, a forlorn figure returning to the only car left in the parking area, to discover, just ten minutes after setting off, that my usual route back to Bristol was completely impassable because of floodwater. I was forced to return to the house. The place was deserted, save for the night security guard who had disappeared to make one of his regular checks somewhere in the building, so I looked around, seeking out a suitable area to settle down for the night.

Joe and Jenny's bedroom was an obvious first choice, since at least there was a reasonable sized bed in there, though as fate would have it, the bed had been up-ended and the room used for equipment storage while we had been filming in another part of the house. I turned my attention to Dog and Duck's Den, a construction in the corner of the room that had not appeared in the original design concept. An earlier suggestion for the characters to learn about the world around them was to watch projected images from under the bed-covers until we decided that it was impractical to have two large, heavy, animatronics who moved around on wheels, jump up onto a mattress, hide under the bed covers and then jump back down again.

The Den was a well-constructed alternative. Dog and Duck could glide in and out with ease at floor level and watch films in their own private cinema. It also provided an excellent retreat for a weary director seeking a decent night's slumber, with a handy duvet at his disposal, surrounded by a thick wall of blankets that offered welcome insulation from the night air.

Except that in the morning when the lighting assistant came into the room to collect some kit, he was assailed by heavy snoring emanating from the Den. He immediately alerted security and the rest of the unit that a tramp had somehow broken in and was occupying Dog and Duck's private domain. I woke to a low hum of concerned voices and peeped cautiously out of my duvet to see a row of feet gathered in the doorway, with an anxious voice suggesting that maybe they should call the police.

There was an air of disbelief when I crawled out from my night-time abode, blinking as I readjusted my eyes to the morning light. Despite a collective sigh of relief, few found the situation amusing. Many even seemed visibly disturbed by such a strange occurrence. It was not one of my most memorable career-defining moments and although it put me on the back foot for a week or two, we did produce thirty excellent shows by the final day of filming, an achievement that could never have been fulfilled without my having the full support and co-operation of the unit, even if they did think I was a little odd.

By late February 2001 I had edited and sound mixed the shows in Norwich and sent the transmission copies to the Network Centre. We crossed our fingers that a third series might be in the offing, or that a new show would be commissioned to take its place, but it was a false hope. Budget cuts meant fewer children's shows were now being made, with more frequent repeats aired due to the rising costs of original production. There was also increasing competition from the new digital channels. ITV children's went into steady decline, leaving the field clear for its biggest rival, CBBC, to reap the benefits. It would be at least a decade before money was invested back into ITV children's programming but it would be too late to save the closure of Dan's department at HTV. When he called to tell me the news in the summer of 2001 I was devastated. The chances of Dan attracting interest in new ideas and raising financial backing as an independent in such a climate were slim and, in any event would involve protracted co-production meetings and long run-in times. He remained full of optimism but I knew it would be the last time we would work together.

Over the eleven years of our association Dan Maddicott had been incredibly loyal and supportive, presenting me with a veritable mountain of interesting, stimulating work unequalled by any other producer. In 2017 he received a BAFTA for his work on *The Clangers*, belated recognition for his extraordinary track record in creating and producing a catalogue of quality ground-breaking, entertaining children's shows. It is a hugely impressive achievement and I find it disappointing that the industry has not fully recognised his contribution in this important area. I can only hope that our broadcasting institutions will eventually come to appreciate the role he has played in helping young children experience the wonders of discovery through fun.

BRANDING IRON

A few weeks later, I was standing on a platform at Peterborough railway station, wondering if my great adventure was finally about to hit the buffers, when my cell phone rang. It was Geoff Blampied from a company called Commercial Breaks at Anglia Television, enquiring if I was available for work. I had never met Geoff, nor indeed been aware that Anglia TV even had a commercials production arm, but it seemed a timely piece of good fortune. He told me that a director who was due to take on a shoot at the end of the week had been incapacitated and someone at Anglia had suggested they might give me a try.

'When could you come in and see us?' he enquired anxiously.

I looked up as the Norwich-bound train pulled into the station just ahead of the Ipswich train that I had been waiting for and immediately abandoned any bullshit response about having to check my diary. 'As long as it takes me to get from Peterborough to Norwich on the train standing in front of me,' I replied.

'Brilliant. I'll put the kettle on.'

And that one brief exchange started a ten-year association with a small team of commercials makers based in Norwich, headed by the creative dynamo that is Chas Lister. Chas had moved to north Norfolk a few years earlier to escape the hurly burly of London life, having established himself as a vibrant presence with the capital's top advertising agencies. He knew all the tricks involved in making widgets look appealing and food look sumptuous, and could conjure up half a dozen workable ideas for any single campaign. We clicked immediately, throwing ourselves into every project, developing storyboard concepts with schoolboy enthusiasm and sharing a mischievous sense of humour at every stage of production. For me it was a complete change of direction. I'd had several years' experience in the conceptualising and marketing of ideas in the corporate sector, but this was completely different; it involved the selling of a product in the space of just thirty seconds and proved a tremendous learning curve.

Much had changed, though, since my first experiences in advertising back in 1965. No longer were advertisers allowed to show attractive models smoking cigarettes at social gatherings on jet cruisers or at mountainside retreats; all advertisements for foods high in fat, salt and sugar were removed from programmes which held particular appeal for children up to the age of 16, and every commercial had to be stringently vetted to ensure it neither offended nor made outrageous or unsubstantiated claims. Chas knew his way around the legalities and stringent guidelines, often arguing his corner if he thought the demands were unreasonable or the conceptual message had been misinterpreted, invariably finding creative alternatives when his objections hit stony ground.

Commercials production still held its challenges despite being put under a microscope, and branding was still as vital to a successful campaign. Ironically, when M&S needed to look closely at their marketing strategy, they called on the sixties icon, Twiggy, to head a major relaunch of their fashion range. It was successful for several years and proved yet again that when you get the branding right you can reap the dividends. For Commercial Breaks, Chas Lister's experience in all areas of product selling was invaluable.

What struck me immediately was the attention to detail he gave to every shot. The lighting style had to complement the product perfectly; the positioning of props had to be precise; the movement of extras through the shot and the delivery of lines by presenters and actors timed to perfection; neither overtly over-selling nor under-selling. I would line up shots and brief the on-screen participants, then stand and watch for what seemed an eternity as the lighting cameraman adjusted and tweaked his lights, then moved them a few inches and adjusted them again. I would wait patiently as Chas moved around the set tinkering with props, moving them around, replacing them, and twisting them in different directions. And if the client or agency rep was in attendance, their observations had to be factored in as well. I would pace up and down as the clock started to run down, turning to Chas occasionally to ask if he was happy. If he stared thoughtfully at the set for more than five seconds I knew he wanted to make more refinements, which gave the cameraman another opportunity to move in and readjust his lights.

With a commercial storyboard comprising somewhere between eight and eighteen carefully crafted shots, it was easy to see how some of the projects took up to two days to complete. On one occasion I filmed a mock rugby match as a metaphor for companies working together as a team, and assembled thirty amateur rugby players one gloomy wet Saturday morning on a playing field just outside Bury St Edmunds. When I told the participants it would take longer to film the thirty-second commercial than it would for them to actually play two matches back-to-back they thought I was kidding. As the morning wore on they became more aggressive with their game play and I found it increasingly difficult to get out of the way as wave after wave of burly fly halves thundered past camera, leaving me breathless, completely soaked, and nursing multiple layers of bruises. I would have fared better playing in the match itself.

The range of commercials we worked on was immense, from garden centres to solicitors, builders' merchants to car dealerships, each requiring a unique approach. When Mark Jewell, the owner of two car salesrooms located in different towns in Suffolk, wanted to promote his second-hand fleet by making the on-screen presentation himself, Chas came up with the idea of filming everything split-screen. Using this technique Mark Jewell would appear as two people in the same shots, as if identical twins, promoting the cars either in the same locations, or in the split locations, the word 'Jewell' being interpreted as 'dual'. With Dan Maddicott no longer being able to present me with mind-boggling challenges, Chas Lister was picking up the baton. Not only was timing important but Mark had to be able to hear his pre-recorded voice from the corresponding take in order to respond – a difficult enough task for a professional actor. But he gave a sterling performance and we found ways around the technical difficulties to produce a thirty second advertising spot that made a huge impact on his car sales.

Apart from people from various walks of life who appeared on camera, there were also the more well known, such as Jim Davidson, who promoted finance deals for anyone having difficulty securing loans, and the boxer Frank Bruno, who lent his iconic image to the Land of Leather franchise, promoting furniture at 'knockout' prices.

Working with Frank was something else. When we first met at a Land of Leather store on the outskirts of Plymouth he was everything I had not expected him to be. The laid back, humble Bruno, usually seen making television appearances smartly attired in tailored suits, was replaced by a more colourful, larger-than-life, alter ego who rattled off jokes non-stop wearing a baseball cap, sunglasses, bright red bomber jacket and trainers, as if he had just breezed in from a Hollywood rap concert. More alarmingly, he did not appear to have brought along the jacket, shirt and tie we had requested for the shoot.

'You did bring a change of clothing with you didn't you, Frank?'

'Course I did, man,' he said, holding up the smallest holdall I had ever seen. 'Me shoes are in there as well.'

I opened up the holdall and pulled out a pair of shoes and three items of clothing that were creased and crumpled almost beyond salvation.

'Wicked eh?' he said, followed by his trademark chuckle.

It was obvious Frank had no appreciation of the lengths we would have to go to in order to make him look remotely presentable. While cameras and lights were being positioned, I sent out search parties to requisition an iron and ironing board, which not only took an age but held up proceedings while we resurrected the scrunched-up fabrics with the application of lashings of water spray and intense heat from an industrial iron.

Whilst Frank was not one of the most natural and intuitive performers I have ever put in front of a camera, he was certainly the most entertaining and had a way about him that endeared him to the crew and general public alike. He could also be incredibly mischievous. One of the scenes involved Frank walking towards camera in a wide shot as he pointed to various sofas and chairs along a predetermined route. I suggested he might start his walk from a little further back for the next take and turned my attention to the cameraman to discuss a reframing of the shot. When I turned back, Frank had disappeared from inside the store and could now be seen standing at the far end of the car park. His personal assistant walked up to me and said 'Frank wants to know if he's gone back far enough.' It was just one in a long line of pranks, culminating in a final scene in which Frank spoke directly to camera, telling the viewers of the 'crazy knock-down prices,' for which he had, without my knowledge, procured a pair of plastic eyeballs that shot out on springs as he laughed his trademark laugh. When you have to endure long filming days and spend so much time waiting around as technicians and designers re-light and re-set shots, it helps enormously to have with you artistes whose patience and sense of humour can make the time appear to pass so much quicker. It was sad to hear that some years later Frank had been sectioned under the Mental Health Act but made a positive recovery, declaring that mental illness was the hardest fight he had ever had. I wish him well. He is a funny, astute individual and one of the most popular sportsmen Britain has produced. The agency had certainly boxed clever in choosing Bruno to spearhead their campaign because his immense public appeal was guaranteed to shift product, which, at the end of the day, was the name of the game.

In truth, large stores were not my favourite venues; the agencies usually had set ideas about how their beds and wardrobes should be presented, the filming days invariably involved shifting heavy furniture about endlessly, and we worked in areas where the general public had access, which made filming a safety hazard because of the cable runs and re-positioning of lights.

Fortunately, the Commercial Breaks production slate was varied and before long we were shooting some fun scenarios for Essex Radio, Jobs Norfolk and Pukka Pies, all now under the watchful eye of Helen

Eisler, a producer who had replaced Geoff, and was keen to establish strong working relationships with clients old and new. Whilst many had a real desire to promote their products, the money wasn't always available, so Chas, Helen and graphic designer Martin Rosten cultivated a new genre of advertising which involved animating photographs and text in a colourful and effective presentation at a fraction of the cost. Although the end results may have had less impact on screen, it overcame the problem of asking clients to spend top-end budgets when they were fighting off the competition and needed to be resourceful.

They were the first ominous signs, however, that commercials production might be in for a rough ride over the next few years and until spending became fashionable again there was little anyone could do to avert an inevitable downturn.

WAYS OF THE WARRIORS

Commercials work dropped off over the winter period, for no other reason than the fact that the seasonal Christmas to New Year transition was traditionally a lean time. With no new commissions in the wind by February I started to consider casting the net wider. With impeccable timing a call came through from Nigel Pope at the BBC asking if I would be interested in directing a new series called *Raven* for BBC Scotland. The show involved a group of youngsters taking on physical and mental tasks in a medieval, mystical hinterland, home to the mysterious Raven, an immortal Scottish warlord, played by James Mackenzie. Mackenzie's human form could shape-shift into a raven at will and summon his young warriors to solve numerous puzzles whilst outwitting his hooded accomplices. Whilst it all sounded enormous fun, something told me it would involve some hefty preparation, since an array of special effects, such as contestants disappearing down magic portals, were part and parcel of the gameplay, and the safety issues were horrendous.

One glance at the project outline should have told me it was likely I could be more at risk than any of the players. Swimming in deep lochs; walking on beams positioned twenty feet off the ground; hooded monks wielding weapons and tossing medallions of fire into the air; swinging blades and sliding metal shields waiting to do their worst on The Way of The Warrior, molten lava flows causing destruction as they burnt their way down mountainsides. Was this an environment I seriously wanted to put myself into?

But this was the BBC. They wouldn't expose me to anything that was *really* dangerous.

Would they?

I read through the programme proposal and sent back my thoughts, with detailed notes on how we might address some of the safety issues and achieve the complex real-time visual effects. By Easter I had packed my bags and was on my way to Glasgow to meet up with the production unit and my co-director Brian Ross. One of our first ports of call was the location where we would be filming the series, in the grounds of Castle Toward, eight miles south-west of Dunoon near Toward Point. To reach it we had to drive to Greenock and catch the ferry to Dunoon, a pleasant enough journey, away from the noise and bustle of the city.

Set designer Tom Barker had already set up camp at Castle Toward and was hard at work building the props, designing the sets and constructing The Way of the Warrior, a corridor of physical obstacles based on the medieval gauntlets of peril that Knights faced as a way of proving their worth. Brian and I made several trips to Castle Toward during the pre-production phase to check out the prop builds and to find suitable locations to film the tasks.

It was, in every respect, the perfect location for *Raven*. The original Castle Toward dates from the 15th century, its fields and woods covering some two hundred and twenty-six acres, with extensive views over the Firth of Clyde. Though much of these natural vistas remained, the original castle itself had fallen into disrepair long ago, leaving a scattering of ruins which provided a suitable backdrop for much of the gameplay. More significantly, Castle Toward in recent times had become an outdoor activity centre, including kayaking, high ropes, and orienteering, as well as gorge walks and hill walks, all supervised by safety experts who would be working closely with us to ensure there were no mishaps.

As we started to schedule the shoot the enormity of what we were taking on hit home. *Raven* incorporated testing gameplay with drama sequences and special effects, spread over an area much wider than we had envisaged, and with many of the locations not accessible by any mode of transport, some potentially hazardous. The design department often had to carry the props, including giant polystyrene boulders and fake trees, over hills and dales, like a small army of ants transporting their worldly possessions. There was also the problem of avoiding filming any twenty-first century images, such as buses, cars, joggers or people walking dogs, which would have to be 'removed' during the edit.

It was initially planned as a two-camera shoot but I campaigned for a third camera because it would allow us better coverage and more options if we needed to split the crew at any point. It seemed a failsafe strategy except that each camera had to send a micro signal to our scanner because it was not possible to connect cables over such vast areas. An electrical supply would have been non-existent in the middle of nowhere anyway and we would rarely have an opportunity to use a generator, even if it was physically possible to cart one around with us. Added to which the scanner was to be situated in a cramped Land Rover which would invariably be sitting in a remote area of wasteland coping with occasional technical dropout because the micro signals would not be able to penetrate walls or bend themselves around trees and hedgerows. The sound recordist had the added problem of monitoring sound input from seven radio mics attached to the actor and the six contestants, who might be wandering anywhere inside that vast terrain at any one time.

I have to admit to feeling immensely pressured when the unit eventually turned up en masse for the first day of the shoot. We had an awesome list of demanding scenes to work our way through, most of a complexity never tried before, and there was so much that we were not a hundred per cent sure about until we started recording - at which point we were assailed constantly by the flesh-hungry midges and sudden changes in weather conditions, from sizzling sunshine to downpours within the space of a few minutes. I recall filming a scene with Raven and five warriors who were standing in pouring rain, whilst the unit comprising wardrobe, make-up and our production manager, stood in a river of mud, huddled under umbrellas. But we had to get it right in order to complete on schedule and set out a workable template for any future series.

James Mackenzie was very patient during the first week of shooting. He wasn't just acting out a role; he had to be alert to how the tasks were progressing, constantly giving encouragement to the players whilst making them aware of the dangers, be they real or fictional. I remember on one occasion, during filming of the High Beam sequence, hearing a continual weeping sound. At first I thought it was one of the camera crew who had had enough and wanted to go home but it turned out to be a contestant who was edging his way along the beam, sobbing inconsolably. I instructed all three cameras to give me wide and medium shots, but no close shots. James asked him if he wanted to come down but the lad was persistent – he was going to finish that task come hell or high water.

After he had successfully crossed the beam we brought him back to ground level and gave him time to recover before laying a beam on the ground and filming a re-enactment, only this time without him sobbing. With the camera shooting from ground level and pointing towards the sky, nobody would know we had filmed a post-trauma insert, which frankly was nothing less than he deserved for his display of audacious courage and tenacity.

Somehow I endured ten days of rigorous filming, including two heart-stopping runs in the Way of the Warrior, our lethal path of spiked swing-balls and swerving axes that I rehearsed with the three cameras, having foolishly undertaken the walk-through myself so that the camera operators could line up their shots and I would have an idea of the difficulties the contestants would face. I skidded, ducked and jigged my way through this torturous path of self-destruction, narrowly avoiding broken ankles and decapitation, but covering my tracks whenever I was knocked off course by pointing out that these were the kind of accidents that we needed to be prepared for.

I elected not to try the Loch Endurance Swim as there was only so much physical misfortune I could court on a shoot, and avoided taking part in rehearsing the jousting contest on the grounds that I had a grossly unfair height advantage over any opponent. With the molten lava flow thankfully being a special effect, I even sidestepped the possibility of being burnt alive before the first shooting period was completed.

So. Did we get it right?

I suppose we must have done, considering the series won a Bafta in its first year of production and spawned many more outings for Raven and his intrepid warriors. Much of the gameplay was subsequently revised and developed, Aisha Toussant taking over from James Mackenzie in a 2018 revamp of the series, but our initial work in establishing the parameters of possibility had proved that *Raven* could succeed despite all the obstacles.

Was it fun? Did I enjoy it?

Well no, for the most part I didn't because it was relentlessly stressful, which is unfortunate because I have always maintained that you should have fun and enjoy working on all your projects, whatever the difficulties. *Raven,* regrettably, is my one career exception.

IT'S A WRAP

When I returned to Suffolk, Commercial Breaks had more work lined up but talk of recession was still ever present and advertising was always one of the first areas to be hit in times of austerity. When there are limited resources it reduces the motivation to invest. For a few years we had been fortunate to work on some interesting projects, but it wasn't to last. The downturn had bitten hard by the end of the first decade of the new millennium and broadcast advertising went into temporary decline.

In the summer of 2004, I took on my final assignment for children's television featuring a mole who lived in a vast underground cavern frequented by other colourful puppet-based characters who told stories and sang songs. The production itself followed a standard puppet-based formula: write scripts, compose music, record songs and voices, tape everything to playback in a studio. Whilst the show had strong production values and was hugely popular with its young audience, there were few moments when I felt it was a rewarding experience. The technical set-up, for a start, involved a pedestal camera operating from the studio floor and a camera mounted on a jib arm. Pedestal cameras are relatively lightweight and mobile and can more or less 'float' around the studio, whilst a camera mounted on a jib arm takes up a ridiculously large amount of space and has to be either trundled or swung into position. I was the only one of the three directors working on the series who declined to use the jib because I regarded it as a cumbersome and unnecessary piece of equipment. The higher the camera goes, the greater the risk there is of revealing the structural parts of the set and the puppeteers themselves, making it, for me, time-consuming and self-defeating.

I preferred to keep my shots at ground level for practical and aesthetic reasons, apart from the fact that with an enormous jib arm taking up valuable floor space, there was a strong likelihood I would spend half my time walking into it and concussing myself. Since my particular shows were sandwiched between the two other directors' schedules, it meant the camera supervisor had to dismantle the jib mount and replace it with a pedestal mount for my session, then piece it all back together again ready for the director who followed me, which did little to elevate my rating in the popularity stakes.

Nature played a decisive role in my next period of misfortune when West London was hit by torrential rain and freak floods that temporarily closed down most of the Tube stations in the area and created roadside lakes that had to be negotiated in order for me to travel between my hotel and the studio on a daily basis. The set had been constructed inside a photographic studio that was not sound-proofed. Under normal circumstances this isn't a problem when puppeteers are miming to playback, but filming becomes impossible when hailstones are clattering on the roof and the puppeteers cannot hear the soundtrack. Added to which, the floodwaters eventually surged in and the technical crew had to unplug everything electrical (which was most of the kit) and move it to a higher level on chairs, tables and cupboards, losing us valuable shooting time.

I thought there was very little that could impede progress after that but I was wrong. During a hairy afternoon session when we were racing to make up for lost time, I heard distressed noises coming from somewhere on the set and halted recording for a closer inspection. It turned out to be one of the puppeteers who had had enough of being stuffed inside the prop sofa for hours on end and wanted out. I couldn't blame him; puppeteers spend inhumane amounts of time crammed into television sets, washing machines, desk drawers and all manner of household appliances during the course of a working day and often become part of a forgotten entourage when the focus is transferred elsewhere. We peeled him away from the upholstery and took the poor chap off for coffee and a biscuit so he could get some feeling back in his arms and legs, whilst I ran a check in my mind on how many actors and technicians over the years must have been reduced to tears at some point on my watch - in many cases, to my shame, in situations I was probably oblivious to.

Suffice it to say, relief rippled noticeably through the entire production team when my filming sessions were finally completed, matched only by my own desire to beat a hasty retreat back into a real world that was not inhabited by characters made of colourful fur with the inclination to burst relentlessly into song every few minutes. I resolved to never again

296

take on work in a studio environment where the sets were built five feet off the ground in order to accommodate a small army of human beings who wave their arms in the air with a fluffy creature of one sort or another attached to their wrists. Children's television in general had lost the appeal it once had and I knew the moment had come to call time on any future projects.

In between less frequent commercials assignments I tutored students at the Met Film School at Ealing Studios – a place I had not been back to since 1968 – as a means of giving something back to an industry that had served me well. A team of highly experienced industry practitioners, headed by the inspirational Jonny Persey, mentored students who came from all walks of life, were of varying ages, nationalities and beliefs, and who had a desire to make films that were either personal to them or simply a means of helping them acquire new sets of skills; artists and writers eager to experiment with an audio visual medium, performers who wanted to show off their skills, journalists seeking to use film to explore important social issues, or people who simply wanted to document events around them and step into a new world of discovery and challenge.

Many of these first-timers made films full of extraordinary insight and creative intensity, some brimming with high entertainment value, others reflecting the students' personal experiences or a need to highlight injustices in an unjust world. One girl had signed up to the course because her brother had been killed in a gang fight and she wanted to investigate the reasons why knife crime had become so endemic; another explored the highs and lows of being a street performer in London's Covent Garden, another took her camera into the little known world of the funeral director, interviewing employees about their personal beliefs on life, death and the possibility of a world beyond. The enthusiasm and passion that these aspiring film-makers poured into their projects opened my eyes to the infinite possibilities that could and should be explored in the filmmaker's quest to look more closely at our diverse multi-cultural planet with fresh eyes and with unique creative expression.

After two years of teaching students from an eclectic mix of backgrounds, the Met Film School gained accreditation to tutor BA courses. In order for me to continue teaching my documentary module I first had to submit details of my academic background to the university. I did not have an academic background; at least not one of any significance to a reputable educational establishment. I left school at the age of sixteen with just two GCE O Levels, and these now looked predictably pathetic holding hands in isolation at the top of the Qualifications section with six inches of empty white space sitting beneath them.

Qualifications were never an issue when I entered the industry in 1964. You just bobbed and weaved your way over the trapdoors, using initiative and survival instincts to elbow your way along, learning the ropes and exuding confidence even at times when you may have suffered moments of self-doubt.

Learning on the job was the name of the game. Today, there are fewer opportunities for apprenticeships of the traditional kind. Camera operators generally work their visual miracles without an assistant, on some occasions recording the sound and positioning the lights themselves; edit assistants no longer hang film trims in trim-bins, because editing now takes place on a laptop computer, courtesy of lightning-speed software and digital timelines. Everything is electronic and traceable and the rushes no longer get scratched to pieces every time they are viewed, the trims being instantly reinstated at the click of a mouse.

I filled in the Qualifications section as best I could: over forty-five years' experience as a film editor, writer and director, working for most of the broadcasting networks; ten years in corporate television tabling suggestions to the boards of giant corporations as to how to apply creative solutions to their communications problems; two years tutoring film students so that they would be better equipped when they ventured into the land of media opportunity.

I was assured it would not be a problem, and it wasn't, I could carry on tutoring. It would have been a huge disappointment if my credentials had not been deemed acceptable, because whilst academic recognition may see students out of the starting blocks, it is hands-on experience, adaptability, commitment, tenacity and aptitude that will propel them over line.

Having been given the green light I spent another two years making frequent visits to this same studio complex where it had all begun for me nearly forty years earlier. The BBC had long since moved out, leaving no trace that they had ever been there; just memories projected onto the walls of my mind as I wandered around trying to place the fading imagery into some kind of perspective. Although the Adventure Unit no longer turned up at the studio gates after their amazing exploits in the steamy jungles of South America, and the Time Machine now stood abandoned and derelict in a corner of the prop store, there was much to be hopeful about. Under new ownership, independent productions were in full gear, cinema films and television dramas occupying the sound stages, giving the country's most famous studios a welcome new lease of life. It was fitting, too, that I should have ended my own big adventure working on commercials, despite the dramatic changes that had taken place since those dim and distant days when Richard Lester, David Bailey and Ken Russell walked the corridors of James Garrett and Partners, full of boundless energy and exhilarating visual ideas.

Everything came full circle on February 24th 2012, when Anglia TV closed down Commercial Breaks, having already mothballed its main sound stage, putting to rest any remaining hope that regional television, apart from news bulletins, might be kept alive until the winds of uncertainty had petered out. The unthinkable and the inevitable finally happened in 2014 when it was announced that Teddington Studios, at one time the beating heart of British commercial television production, was to be razed to the ground and replaced by a 213-apartment development complex. It was devastating news for those of us who held such fond memories of these celebrated and much loved facilities, where artistes like Benny Hill, Morecambe and Wise, Frankie Howard, Tommy Cooper and Michael Bentine once entertained us with their unique brand of comedy, and such popular shows as *Bless This House, Men Behaving Badly, Callan, Man at the Top, Opportunity Knocks, Rumpole of the Bailey* and *Rock Follies* held their audience ratings for months on end.

Whilst the aforementioned performers and shows are, for the most part, from a bygone era, Teddington studios was nevertheless in full production up until December 2014 making contemporary classics such as *Mr Bean, The Office, The IT Crowd, TV Burp and Not Going Out,* all drawing huge acclaim and making it difficult to fathom why, at a time when entertainment and drama productions were in such high global demand, better use could not have been made of such a historic complex, particularly as 2016 was a boom year for high end TV production, generating a record £478 million inward investment - an impressive 11 per cent increase on the previous year. Yet Teddington was just one of many casualties, along with HTV West in Bristol and Anglia in Norwich, where I had been afforded the opportunity to carve a career for myself in one of the most vibrant and exciting industries on earth.

My magic carpet is a little frayed around the edges now and no longer takes me on those wonderful journeys that fashioned my youth and shaped my future; a voyage of discovery I was fortunate and privileged to be a part of. I had worked on some of broadcasting's most iconic programmes, alongside some of the very best the industry had to offer and pioneers of varying genres. Not just famous people like Laurence Olivier, Lenny Henry and Hughie Green, but also ordinary, inspirational folk of immense courage and conviction, like the mountaineer Mick Burke and the skier Mike Nemesvary. I was, without doubt, extremely lucky to be part of such an extraordinary odyssey, even though to some extent I did lead a charmed life; not so much walking on water as running across hot coals, but somehow surviving my baptisms of fire, even if I did get my fingers burnt occasionally.

Today's filmmakers have different sets of challenges to face as they fly about on digital, three-dimensional magic carpets that take them on new quests, fashioning ground-breaking ways of telling stories and making observations about the planet we occupy that make us think about our relevance in society whilst encouraging us to participate in every way possible.

The creative arts have weathered many storms, informing and entertaining us whilst offering hope in times of adversity and giving us reason to believe that our minds will continue to be opened to the endless possibilities that lie in wait along the ever-changing information highway.

At least now I can watch from the safety of my armchair, away from the trapdoors that others will need to discover in order to make their own adventures in the world of broadcast production interesting and rewarding, affording them the

302

privilege of becoming part of the remarkable journey that television has taken since those early transmissions back in my youth, when programmes were transmitted in black and white on TV sets with wires that over-heated, valves that burnt out regularly and a roof aerial that caused the picture to judder and shift in and out of focus whenever an aeroplane passed overhead, the budgie escaped from its cage, or the next-door neighbours started shouting obscenities at each other.

I marvel at the road broadcasting has travelled and the momentous achievements it has made. At worst it has the ability to cheapen human endeavour and be self-indulgent, but at its best it can be truly inspirational. Television can transport us to places both real and fictional that heighten our awareness of the world, stimulate our senses, and help keep alive the spirit of community that was so important to so many before the magic box came along to transform our lives forever.

INDEX

45095597R00177

Printed in Poland
by Amazon Fulfillment
Poland Sp. z o.o., Wrocław